Professional Ethics

&

Functional Behavior

(Islamic Theory)

Presented by:

Dr. AGHADEER SALEM ALIDROOS

Associate Professor Department of Educational Administration and Planning

Umm Al Qura University

Introduction

Authors may not write any book unless in the following sections: Write about something new which has never been composed about, something which is not completed, write to explain an impenetrable thing, to summarize lengthy works, correct something wrong or to collect information about one subject" *[*]).

This good tip uttered by Azhari scientist of the seventeenth century is always retains its value and calling every writer to follow its approach.

The conscious reader shall estimate the extent to which our book, offered now, fulfill such provisions.

This book about code of ethics and worker behavior is not just a work but it is trying to submit these provisions set out by the mentioned Azhari scientist.

This book seeks to gather information that may be necessary for code of ethics and worker behavior which represent basic for all successful works as there is no point of any civilized progress not based on moral grounds. In this book, we tried to highlight that morality improves behavior and acts, and these acts and behavior brighten the personality up as the worker personality varies from one person and another as a result of variation in behavior. The worker behavior shall be subject to a rule called "**Obligation**" which we seek to be achieved by this book, obligation with code of ethics that contribute to develop human resources in order to produce works effectively. The absence of the concept of positive work ethics is an element affecting negatively on human development which reflects negatively on implementing development programs in the economic, social and organizational aspects.

Since we are aware that many books and researches addressed this subject theoretically, I seek, in this book, to cover something new (invented) like an administrative philosophy to be a practical mechanism for applying these morals in worker behavior. Obligation with code of ethics shall be a responsibility followed by a penalty. Such responsibility based on obligation, in case the obligation being missed, responsibility shall be missed accordingly and if responsibility being missed justice and rights shall be lost. Therefore, we address and explain

---

[*] Shamsuddin Al-Babil, deceased in 1077 AH, mentioned by Mohammed Abdullah Draz in the book "The Constitution of Quran" (1973).

[*] In this subject; we will quote the following Ayat from the Holy Quran: Al-Baqarah: 25, 62, 82, 277; An-Nisa: 57, 132, 173; Al-Maidah: 9, 93, 69; Al-Anam: 48; Al-Araf: 42; Yunus: 4, 9; Hud: 23; Ar-Rad: 29; Ibrahim: 23; Al-Kahf: 30, 88, 107; Maryam: 60, 96; Ta-Ha: 82; Al-Hajj: 14, 23, 50, 56; An-Nur: 55; Al-Furqan: 70; Ash-Shuraa: 277; Al-Qasas: 67, 80; Al-Ankabut: 8, 9, 58; Ar-Rum: 15, 45 and Luqman: 8.

what stated theoretically and set out this administrative philosophy and formulate it in an implementable Islamic theory. This book also shall be workable to form controls to establish Islamic ethics for staff so, this book gathers between theory and practice under the Islamic law.

This book contains five chapters. Chapter one addresses the concept of ethics and its purpose, behavior, personality and relationship between ethics and behavior. Chapter two addresses code of ethics; the profession concept in job and with staff, ethics and functional behavior values, sources of this professional behavior, ethical practices in Saudi Systems. Chapter three addresses administrative corruption and functional deviation, clearing the administrative corruption standards, reasons, affects and methods of treatment. Chapter four addresses work ethics and worker ethics in Islam, clearing the difference between ethics, faith and work in Islam. Chapter five addresses ethics formatting and administrative corruption from Islam point of view. The practical side is formulating the Islamic theory to compose ethics using administrative audit strategy which is the administrative corruption treatment mean.

The author is keen to simplicity, clearance and logical sequence.

We hope that the book achieves the expected benefit, and the book's benefit spread throughout all staff, employers and students and applying. Allah the Highest says: {He sends down water from the sky and the valleys (Wadis) flow each in their measure, and the torrent carries a swelling scum; and fire from that which they kindle; desiring ornament or ware, from that rises a scum like it. As such, Allah strikes both the truth and the false. As for the scum it is cast away as jetsam, but, that which profits people remains on the earth. As such Allah strikes the parables} (Ar-Ra'd: 17) Allah almighty has spoken the truth.

Author:

Dr. Aghadeer Salem Al-Aidroos

(Chapter One)

Ethics and Behavior

Chapter One:

Ethics and Behavior

1. Ethics concept

2. Purpose of commitment with ethics

3. Meaning of behavior

4. Overall objective of behavior

5. Importance of good behavior

6. Ethics and behavior

7. Behavior and personality

Ethics

1. Ethics concept:

Nations and people's progress throughout the ages is related to values and ethics practiced in real life. Human life cannot be continued regularly unless by behavioral controls to regulate people's relationships. Ethics represents the most important controls that urged by divine legislation and it is the first pillar to save nations and its evolution, accordingly, work ethics studying shall have a great importance for various sectors in the society.

Since morality is the basis for human behavior in societies, we could explain the concept of morality through three aspects: the language meaning, ethics in philosophy and from an Islamic perspective.

Lexical meaning:

(Ibn Manzoor, 1993) defined morality as follows: "Morality is the religion, impression and nature. It represents human inside and have good and bad aspects." (p. 194)

Convention meaning:

(Ibn Maskaweh, D. T) defined morality as follows: morality is the personality status expressed by its actions without thinking. This status divided into: a natural one such as a push for a person who is bad-tempered and the other status is derived from customs and training that executed after careful thought then the person continue to practice this morality step by step till it became his own morality." (P. 41)

(Al-Saud & Bettah, 1996) defined morality as: "A rule or rules of behavior practiced by a person who lives in a group." (P. 302)

Osman (1405 AH, p. 36) defines ethics as: "Usual and known behavior, and a person with ethics is practicing virtue and acts in a right way."

Ethics can be defined as: "Moral principles of a particular tradition, group, or individual. Individuals use their believe in values, customs and traditions acquired by members of a society from good, right and justice in organizing their affairs in this society through acting a certain behavior in a situation. It is the general framework which directs the human behavior."

2. Ethics in philosophy:

Ethics concept for philosophers emanates from their principles in which they believe. Each philosopher defined moral meaning and properties according to his philosophy principles. Ethics definition in philosophy can be explained as summarized by "Yaljehin" (1413 AH, 35-42) as follows:

First Attitude: Descriptive Social Approach:

According to Yaljehin, there are three meanings for the word "Ethics":

1. The word "Ethics" shall be for a set of ideas, judgments, emotions and habits related to people's rights and duties towards each other which is accepted and recognized in some civilization or era.

2. The word "Ethics" shall be for a science that studies these phenomena.

3. The word "Ethics" shall be for this science application, as justice, cooperation and security derived from the progress in morality.

In light of this approach, Ethics is a descriptive realistic science which studies human behavior according to time and place, not a standard perfect science (considering what is actually done). "Levy Yazal" believes in this approach.

Second attitude: Standard Mental Approach in Defining Ethics:

This trend describes moral as the perfect human behavior according to ideals which have to be followed by the human mental in the behavior because it is a duty, not a target. According to this approach, moral is a standard science not a descriptive science. Socrates, Aristotle and Plato were believe in this approach and thought that moral is a target or purpose.

Third Attitude: Utilitarian Approach:

This approach contains three principles as follows:

1. Personal Pleasure: it is the pleasure and happiness for human (i.e. happiness is pleasure). This principle's owners thought that the individual have to seek of pleasure and avoid pain. Individual behavior that achieves such happiness based on pleasures is an ethical conduct. One of this principle's owners is "Aristo" who is "Socrates" pupil.

2. Utilitarianism: One of this principle's owners is "Hobbs". According to this principle; human nature is selfish that maximizes utility of self. Human has created moral principles as a way to achieve benefit.

3. Pragmatism: Presented by (John Dewey). Considers the practical effects of the objects and its moral value unlike utilitarianism, which converts work into commercial and industrial business, and ethics are provided to achieve personal desires rather than being a humanitarian action and social work.

Forth Attitude: Human Nature Approach:

This approach calls ethics as "Human Attributes Science". Ethics definition therefore is "individual behavior principles derived from human nature". From this principle's followers

"Adam Smith & Hanshion" and also followed by Jean-Jacques Rousseau who thought that the human nature itself is good but the country spoiled this nature.

According to this approach; moral principles could be derived from Human Attributes.

Ethics for Greek is a humanitarian science based on philosophers' perspectives; the most famous philosophers who wrote about moral are as follows:

* **Socrates**: wrote about virtue and considered that virtue is knowledge while immorality is an acquaintance. Its mission was focusing on bring the attention of his followers to the necessity of subordinate their beliefs and practical actions for mental criticism. Knowledge according to Socrates is the basis of wisdom and wisdom is the way to the sound moral. The inner knowledge of soul is in the forefront of these knowledge because inner knowledge, in its nature, is good and knowing its capabilities make human to realize his\ her position from others so that, your relationship with them will be right.

* **Plato**: understood the human conscience well and did not call it with its real name, Plato was not distinguishing between conscience and mind. There is no one defined or described conscience better than Plato. Plato has been tried to address an organized perspective about nature, God and man then he and deduced moral principles.

Plato believes that human must overcome body's demands to live a good life but may satisfy such physical needs in order to achieve body stability while focusing one's interest on self-corroborated. In order to achieve the same, the individual must direct him\ herself knowledge and wisdom acquisition. This approach may free the soul from the body prison in this life so that, the soul could contact with ideal world and living life of virtue similar to life after death (i.e. the life that is disinterested in desires and instincts). Human should not lead an ascetic life, but shall suppress soul and overcome it to achieve his\ her virtuous humanity by wisdom.

* **Aristotle**: wrote three books about ethics as follows:

1. Great Ethics' science.

2. Ethics' science to Oudium

3. Ethics' science to Nicomajos

Aristotle philosophy of ethics starts from a base that defined the individual as: "A person who is civilian and friendly by nature". This instinct makes the individual being exited to meet with others and this interest drives him to seek integration capabilities and secure needs necessary to achieve community and individual happiness. Happiness based on sound biography and good work is a purpose in human community.

<u>**3. Ethics in the contemporary thought:**</u>

Ethics perspectives in non-Islamic thought can be summarized as follows:

*** Marxism:** Argue that existence is just the visible physical world and the economic factor is the only factor that runs the human in life. Marxist position accordingly rejects all moral values and abstract meanings totally and on top of high values are (Religion).

*** Pragmatism:** One of the most prominent pioneers of this theory is "William James". Ethics according to William James is championship, fight and role assigned to the individual as human role in life shall not be negative but must prove its existence. One of this theory's principles is that performance and works cannot be measured by its principles even by its consequences results.

*** Existentialism:** Its basic premise is that human should make him\ herself as axis thinking. Ethics according to this theory is based on two principles: Atheism and Human Freedom.

The first principle: reject Theism totally as they consider that Theism is a kind of restriction on freedom while Human Freedom (The second principle) according to Existentialism means total rejection of what could be called rule, principle or law because the individual morality nature does not accept any restriction come from outside soul.

* There is theory which argues that the environment around youth, women and children in social systems shall be suitable in order to amend individual. New researches addressed rights, duties and informing individual with greatness of responsibility towards the community and him\ herself.

* "Immanuel Kant" the German philosopher developed a book entitled "Metaphysics Foundations of Ethics" as he considered all the work without conscience revelation, power of free will and voice of absolute order abstract from any objectives is not a good work.

* Other writers such as "Descartes, Malebranche and Spinoza" who represents a principle called "Metaphysics of Ethics" on the grounds that the universe consistence and harmony which have known target and planned approach shall be applied on human nature.

* The most important scientists who addressed morality are: "Paul Foulquié, Juliqih and Lucien"

- (Paul Foulquié) defined morality as: "Code of conduct group which shall be considered by the individual in order to reach his\ her goal."

- (Juliqih) defined morality as: "Science that argues the appropriate use of human freedom in order to achieve the end goal."

- (Lucien) defined morality as: "Total of uneven pattern of ideal selections, rules and goals that must be achieved by individual through his\ her work in the life to increase the value of life."

* Morality is: "Set of rules and values that control the proper conduct of the individual and communities."

* (Ahmed Amin) defined morality as: "Science that explaining the meaning of good and evil, and shows how people should treat with each other."

* (Omaia Badran) defined ethics as: "Normative science addresses rules and principles that control the human behavior and assess his\ her conduct based on such rules."

4. Ethics in the context of Islamic Thought:

Islamic thought interested in morality and Islamic teachings was, still and will remain a call for noblest morals completeness forever to achieve humanity happiness in both world and hereafter.

(Al-Ghazali) in his book "Revival of Religious Sciences" about morality, he found that moral is: "The well-established part in the soul that can easily show acts with no need to ideology and deliberately. In case such part shows good acts it can be called good moral and if acted in a bad way it can be called bad moral"(p. 505).

(Yaljehin 1992 AD, 74) defined Islamic ethics as: "Science of good and evil, beauty and ugly. It is one of the most important Islamic sciences which based on sources of Islamic knowledge including Holy Qur'an, Sunnah and other legislative sources."

(Al Mzgagi, 1994) indicates that Islamic ethics mean: "set of lawful values, which Muslim (official) have and have clear effect on both private and public behavior, achieving goodness, preventing evil, backing up right, resisting vain, supporting justice and good and rejecting injustice and tyranny in the community in the light of certain rules and standards control this behavior" (p. 251).

Moreover, others also defined Islamic ethics as: "set of sayings and deeds should be based on fundamental concepts, rules, virtues, and decencies connected closely with creed and Islamic religious law through Quran and Sunna Islam is a creed, law and ethics integrated with each other's".

Ethics have great importance in Islam for individual and community as ethics is the basic of setting all deeds and warships, which person performs, right for it is the path for achieving man's happiness in the world and the hereafter. Prophet Mohamed -PBUH- says about that: **{Nothing is heavier on the believer's Scale on the Day of Judgment than good character. For indeed** Allah, **Most High, is angered by the shameless obscene person}** (Sunan Abu Dawoad, Al-Tirmidhi, Sahih Al-Tirmidhi, part (8), the book of Righteousness And Maintaining Good Relations With Relatives, page: 167), this narration refers to the importance of the man's good ethics. (Al Mzgagi, 1994, p. 255) indicates that ethics are considered as a main pillar of man's happiness for no ethics in a non-ethical community but also no righteousness or setting right for it. Islam concerned for this important aspect and made it as the best path to the dealing based on solidarity, compassion, harmony, and peace among individuals and groups. Allah praises his prophet -PBUH- in Quran where for his behavior and characteristics (Ethics) saying: **{And indeed, you are of a great moral character}** (AL-QALAM, 4). Good manner is one of things Islam urged on and this is indicated in ethics' rank in Quran and Sunna where verses and Hadith are repeated to praise good manner in various positions such as, Allah the Highest says: **{And among those we created is a community which guides by truth and thereby establishes justice}** (AL-A'RAF, 181) and Allah the Highest also says: **{Indeed, this Qur'an guides to that which is most suitable and gives good tidings to the believers who do righteous deeds that they will have a great reward}** (AL-ISRA, 9).

- Prophet Mohamed -PBUH- says when he was asked: **{ the Messenger of Allah was asked about that for which people are admitted into Paradise the most, so he said:**
- **{Taqwa of Allah and good character.}** (Narrated by Imam Ahmed in his Musnad and Al-Tirmidhi, "2003").
- Prophet Mohamed -PBUH- says: **{A believer will attain by his good behavior the rank of one who prays during the night and observes fasting during the day}** (Narrated by Imam Ahmed in his Musnad, "24620").
- Prophet -PBUH- says: **{The most perfect believer in respect of faith is he who is best of them in manners.}** (Narrated by Imam Ahmed in his Musnad, "10106").
- Prophet -PBUH- says: **{Indeed I have only been sent to complete the noble qualities of morals}** (Narrated by Imam Malik in Muwatta "3357", authenticated by Imam Ahmed in Musnad "8729").

- In Hadith narrated by the mother of the believers Mrs. Aisha (May Allah be pleased with her) says: **{His character was the Qur'an}** (in Al-Musnad A-jamea, authenticated by Ahmed "91\6"), it means that prophet Mohamed was adhering to Quran and its decencies, orders, prohibitions, and what is included in the Quran of generosities and good manners.

Islam that came to complete man's generosities of ethics is distinguished to be interested in this matter that Islam is interpreted as being moral religion. Allah the Highest says: **{And indeed, you are of a great moral character}** (AL-QALAM, 4). Moreover, Ibn Abas (May Allah be pleased with him) said: Islam is a great religion.

This will be clear through the following important facts:

- Close connection between faith as a doctrine and ethics as a behavior for ethics is a sign of the complete faith; as long as the goodness of morals increased, the degree of the believer increased. Prophet -PBUH- said: **{The dearest and the closest of you to me on the Day of Resurrection will be those who are the best in behavior}** (Authenticated by At tabarani in the Al-Sagheer and Al-Awsat, Al Mughnl "part (1), 1\932"), and Allah the Highest says: **{O you who have believed, fear Allah and be with those who are true}** (AT-TAWBAH, 119). In Hadith too: **{A man is not a believer who fills his stomach while his neighbor is hungry}** (Was narrated by Al-Bukhari, in Al-Adab Al-Mofrad "112"and Al- Tabarani in Al-Kabeer "3\175").

- Warships that have an ethical effect must be achieved in the group life and these are some examples:

- **{Recite, [O Muhammad], what has been revealed to you of the Book and establish prayer. Indeed, prayer prohibits immorality and wrongdoing, and the remembrance of Allah is greater. And Allah knows that which you do}** (AL-'ANKABUT, 45), as prayer prohibits every immorality and wrongdoing such as, theft, adultery and drinking alcohol.....etc.

- **{Take, [O, Muhammad], from their wealth a charity by which you purify them and cause them increase, and invoke [Allah's blessings] upon them. Indeed, your invocations are reassurance for them and Allah is Hearing and Knowing}** (AT-TAWBAH, 103). It is also a purification of soul of the moral of stinginess or withhold.

- **{There is [to be for him] no sexual relations and no disobedience and no disputing during Hajj}** (AL-BAQARAH, 197), pilgrimage prohibits immoral saying, grave disobedience deeds and useless talk which don't lead but to dispute, fight and bigotry; especially in pilgrimage.
- Ethics are a condition of dealings validation. Allah the Highest says :**{ O you who have believed, do not consume one another's wealth unjustly but only [In lawful] business by mutual consent. And do not kill yourselves [or one another]. Indeed, Allah is to you ever Merciful}** (AN-NISA, 29). This business shall be by satisfaction and without gambling or exploitation during fund transactions. Allah the Highest says: **{Woe to those who give less [than due]}** (AL-MUTAFFIFIN, 1) and prophet -PBUH- says: **{he who cheats us is none of us}** (Authenticated by Ibn Hayan "1107", Al-Tabarani in Al-Kabeer, part (10)\ No. 10234). When dealing with weighted goods, we must commit with fairness in weights and not to cheat.
- Islamic penalties are prohibitions of moral crimes (Penalty of murder, theft and adultery). The penalties approved by Islam indicate its concerning towards ethics to protect virtue and good morals. The one who thinks carefully about it realizes that Islam is a creed, law and ethics integrated with each others.

1- **Ethics importance and aim**:

Man's life doesn't go right unless there are behavioral controls organizing people's relations. One of the most important controls is ethics which Islamic religious law urged in both Quran and Sunna, as we mentioned before, for the aim of committing with ethics is to achieve happiness either inside or outside soul.

(Yaljehin, 2002, page: 7-9) mentioned that ethics importance appears in the following:

1- Ethics is one of the best and most honored sciences.
2- Ethical behaviors and decencies distinguish man's behavior of animal's behavior.
3- Ethics' aim is to achieve happiness in the life of individual and group.
4- Ethics is a mean for man's success in life.
5- Ethics is an important mean to promote the nation.

Furthermore, the importance of ethics steam from being the reference frame which directs the behavior of individual and community. In addition, it is the base of the righteousness of all works and warships performed by individual to achieve happiness in world and hereafter.

The importance of this appears in all life fields for its effective influence on the efficiency of the workers of different professions and of course on their production. Both of (Al-Saud & Bettah, 1996) mention that rules, regulations and systems are enough unless they combined with minimum commitment when the state applies them. (Aokla, 1986) sums up ethics' aims for the individual and the community as follows:

- **<u>Ethics aims for the individual</u>**:
  o Changing man to the best.
  o Distinguishing Muslim and his character's independence.
  o Achieving man's happiness through gaining Allah' pleasure and achieving the benefit for the group.
  o Granting man completion and disciplining and purifying soul.
  o Forming the balanced character.
  o Revival of man's conscience and feeling of permanent observation.
  o It is the result of all aims of Islamic religious law in its various aspects.
  o Global education of the individual.
- **<u>Ethics aims for the group:</u>**
  o Building a charitable and virtuous community.
  o Strengthening brotherhood ties, insuring community power and forming awareness of the unity of social life.

Therefore, (Zagzog, 1993, 21) confirms that ethics science study, religiously or philosophical, has a great benefit to guide human's behavior and direct it towards moral values and high ideals upon the base of the deep understanding and recognition. In addition, (Abdeen and Puraai, 1987, 174) add that ethics is the pillar of nation and its symbol among other nations. How many nations deteriorated and declined and even was abolished because it didn't maintain its ethics and deviated towards the path of lust and desires. Good management and behavior depends in so far on ethics, if the employees and officials don't have the meaning of management and peace. Messenger of Allah -PBUH- is a good example for us as he concerned of strengthen the pillars of ethics in community. Prophet says: Prophet -PBUH- says: **{Indeed I have only been sent to complete the noble qualities of morals}** (Was narrated by Imam Malik in Muwatta "3357", Ahmed "2\381").

Based on the foregoing, it indicates the importance of adhering ethics sayings and deeds as there is no use of any civilized, social, political or economical progress for individual or community unless it is bases on moral basis. Messenger of Allah established a state based on a long struggle against many enemies and here he states that the most acceptable deed in their scales in Judgment Day is the goodness moral which proves ethics' rank in Islam.

We can abstract as follows:

- Morals steams from human soul, so it is an accompanied characteristic.
- Morals' connection with human soul is a reason of defaming or praising it depending on being good or bad.
- As morals are related to a status connected with the human soul, therefore, moral is natural disposition or gained and that is why ethics can be improved and promoted.
- Ethics is a main pillar of man's happiness and nations, its basis and civilization because ethics is the basis of setting all deeds and warships performed by man right.
- Islamic ethics is a sign of complete faith when goodness of morals increase, the degree of faith increases as well. Prophet -PBUH- says:**{The nearest among you to me will be one who is the best of you in manners}** (Authenticated by Al-tabarani in Al-Awsat and Al-Sagheer, Al-Mughni book "part (1), 1\932"). The nearest one to the prophet in his council will learn more from him and apply what he learned, so his behavior will be related to the behavior of the one who has the best manners on earth "the prophet". In other words, the one who follows the steps of the prophet will learn righteousness in all deeds.
- Ethics is a behavioral guidance for the soul which directs the individual and communities' behavior. The one who will be the nearest of the prophet will have his ethics as his guidance and as a result, he will have the best manners.

Behavior

1- Definition of behavior:

Behavior: is a source by which action or reaction is called in order to impose something is usually related to the surrounding environment. Behavior can be conscience or unconscious, voluntary or compulsory (Wikipedia).

Human behavior: Are all acts and activities which man does whether they are apparent or hidden. Others define it as: any activity man does whether they are acts can be noticed and measured such as, physiological and dynamic activities or unnoticeable activities such as, thinking, remembering, intellectual obsession and others. Moreover, some people defined behavior as responses man shows as a result of dealing with other or connecting with the external environment. Therefore, behavior includes all what man does such as, dynamic work, thinking, talking, feelings or emotions.

Furthermore, human behavior can be defined as the intellectual, psychological and dynamic response which man shows or performs in his daily life. Intangible activities include thinking, mediation and recognition while the tangible ones include movement, eating, verbal responses and body language.

It can be said that behavior isn't fixed but changes and occurs in a certain environment. Moreover, it may happen accidentally and naturally such as, breathing or coughing or by choice, intentionally and consciously. This behavior can be learnt and affect by environment factors where the individual lives.

Types of behavior:

In general, behavior is divided into two types:

    A- Respondent behavior.

    B- Operant behavior.

A- Respondent behavior: is the behavior which is controlled by stimulants which satisfies and as soon as they occur, behavior occurs. Milk in baby's mouth leads to the production of saliva, tears is dropping during cutting onion and so on. Stimulants before behavior are called pro-stimulants. The respondent behavior is not affected by stimulants follow it, and it is closer to involuntary behavior. If man put his hand in hot water, he will automatically pull it. This behavior is fixed and but what changes are the stimulants which control this behavior.

B- Operant behavior: is behavior which is defined through the environmental factors, such as economic, social, educational, religious, geographical factors and others. Moreover, operant behavior is restricted to its results for posteriori stimulants may weaken or strengthen operant behavior or may not have any effect. We can say that operant behavior is closer to voluntary behavior. Some researchers classified human behavior into categories to facilitate the matter as follows:

- **Natural disposition behavior**: behavior arising with man's creation, such as breathing, eating and drinking.
- **Gained behavior**: behavior that man acquired from the surrounding environment, such as language, religion, customs, traditions and values.
- **Apparent behavior**: behavior appears clearly and can be heard and watched.
- **Hidden behavior**: behavior depends on mind and can't be seen or heard, such as thinking, remembering and imagining.
- **Positive behavior**: behavior consists with religious, moral, social and organizational values.
- **Negative behavior**: behavior disagrees with religious, moral, social and organizational values.
- **Individual behavior**: behavior conducted by one individual.
- **Group behavior**: behavior conducted by a group of people and characterized by power and effect.
- **Deeds behavior**: behavior takes the form of tangible acts and deeds.
- **Verbal behavior:** behavior depends on the language, such as sayings, arguments and dialogues.
- **Remunerative behavior**: behavior achieves the individual's aim as the dedicated employee when gets a reward.
- **Frustrated behavior**: behavior doesn't achieve the individual's aim when gets a reward.
- **Defensive behavior**: behavior which individual practices to defend himself when he fails in achieving his aim or when his behavior is unacceptable by others and this kind has many types.

Behavior characteristics:

1- **Predictable.**

2- **Controllable.**

3- **Measurable.**

1- Predictable: human behavior isn't a spontaneous phenomenon and doesn't happen accidentally. It subjects to certain system and if science can define the elements and components of this system, it will be predicable. Behaviorists think that the environment represented in past and present financial and social circumstances of the person decide his behavior. Therefore, we can predict person's behavior if we knew his previous and present environmental circumstances. When our knowledge of those circumstances increases objectively, our capability to predict behavior increases but this doesn't mean that we can fully predict behavior as we can't know all the surrounding environmental circumstances in the past or in the present.

2- Controllable: "control" in behavior modification usually includes organizing or reorganizing the environmental events which are before or after behavior. Moreover, "auto control" in behavior modification means that person behave himself by using principles and laws used to behave others. The wanted control from behavior modification is the positive control not the negative one. So, the most important method which workers commit with in behavior modification is to increase the method of enhancement and decrease the method of punishment.

3- Measurable: because human behavior is complicated for part of it is apparent, noticeable and measurable and the other part is hidden and can't be measured directly, so scientists didn't agree upon one theory to explain the human behavior.

<u>**Effective factors on behavior**</u>:

    1- Gender (female- male)

    2- Age

    3- Personality

    4- Heredity

    5- Environment

1- <u>Gender (Female- male)</u>: male is not like female as mentioned in Quran when Allah the Highest says: **{And the male is not like the female}** (ALI 'IMRAN, 36). There are behaviors related to female only, such as pregnancy, delivery, feeding and others. Moreover, there are behaviors usually restricted to female like custody of children, nursing, and household chores ....etc. On the other hand, male performing works almost are restricted upon him like leadership, crises management, wars and works need to muscularity, such as construction and infrastructure works.....etc.

2- <u>Age</u>: persons behave according to their age and physical, mental, health, cultural statuses and others. Baby needs private care as he can't take care of himself, talk or act alone. Then, he becomes a boy, teenager and next be young man when behavior through those stages can be prescribed with rush, enthusiasm and immaturity. When he becomes an adult man, then middle-aged and next an old man, then behavior in those stages can be prescribed with wisdom, prudence, and maturity.

3- **Personality**: personality plays an important role in individual's behavior as there are individual differences among persons according to their personalities. Sociable behaviors differ from introverted behaviors, strong than weak, democratic than bossy, attractive personality than confused personality and positive personality than negative personality.

4- **Heredity**: individual's behavior affected by its hereditary characteristics as those characteristics transfer from parents to children by hereditary genes. The effect of heredity on the individual appears clearly through many aspects, including but not limited, physical aspects, such as tall, short, complexion, thinness and obesity, psychological aspects, such as anxiety, introversion and depression and mental aspects, such as intelligence, thinking and recognition. Therefore, individual's behavior affects by those things positively or negatively.

5- **Environment**: environment has a huge effect upon the individual's behavior. Individual acquired his language, beliefs, customs and traditions from the surrounding environment. Moreover, family plays a huge role in bringing up individual with the social, economic and political regime. Environment also affects individuals' behaviors through geographical and climatic aspects. Residents of cold areas have their own behaviors which can be applied upon the residents of hot, temperate, desert, coastal and mountainous areas.

Ethics and behavior:

Ethics: is an endowment of the soul through which man acts without diligence, thinking or vision occur. (At taloaa, 1995, 17) mentions that ethics is that science study as follows:

1- Behavior guidelines.

2- Issuing ethical rules.

It also refers that ethics is considered as a social study for customs, traditions and behavior patterns existed in society. Ethics directs and controls individuals' behavior towards each others. Ethics' rules and functions arise from society. (Frankcna, 1963, P. 6).

Philosophical encyclopedia indicated that the term of ethics generally refers to three meanings related to each others:

1- **General pattern of life style.**

2- **Collection of rules related to behavior.**

3- **Research about life styles and behavior principles (Edwards, 1967, P. 81).**

Behavior: all acts and activities of individual whether they were apparent or hidden. Those acts and activities are controlled, defined and guided by ethics. Ethics is a rule controls, defines and guides behavior.

Behavior
Ethics

scientific methods and right research techniques in order to discover and establish general standards and principles that control the practical practice for achieving virtues and human values and morals. Ethics studies behavior principles and how to rule and control those principles practically. Ethics apply values practically in human life through human behavior. Based on the above, we can say that ethics is generally connected to human behavior. (At taloaa, 1995) says that Ethics is a term includes certain phrases, values and acts man should apply in his life. "Morals" means a habit and repetition of a certain deed. Ethics exists where man exists and distinguishes him as a rational being than other creatures. This distinguish is known through his behavior which means that we judge upon man (According to Ethics) through his behavior. Man is a moral being aims naturally to achieve his rational character through the rational constructive behavior and he always tries to prove this through his behavior and conducts and that he is seeking the best and achieving the planned aim. Man expresses himself when acting through behavior and doesn't achieve his aim unless practicing ethical practical principles which he depend on. This practical practice appears through his behaviors and deeds.

Therefore, both (Parpos & Stock, 1969) said that Aristotle defined the aim of ethics science as it does not lie in understanding but in guiding and improving the practical life. It doesn't aim only to the abstract truth but it aims to the truth that serves the human action and behavior (p.70).

Consequently, ethics is what improve the types of behavior and deeds and it can also criticize and reject other (Types of behavior and deeds). Those deeds and behavior show man's character.

<u>**Behavior and personality**</u>:

Personality: means appearance and making clear in front of others.

Personality is also known as: those relatively continuing and coordinated patterns in recognition, thinking and sensing. It is a stenographic formation including thoughts, motivations, passions, tendencies and others which give people their distinguished character. Personality is a set of qualities, characteristics and traditions which person is characterized by and distinguished with. So, we find that every person is characterized by qualities, characteristics restricted to him and certain customs and rituals that constitute a part of his independent character. To know or judge any person, must notice by his personality through behavior observing (His conducts and deeds).

Therefore, there are individual differences among persons in their personalities appears through their behaviors. Sociable behaviors differ from introverted behaviors, strong than weak, democratic than bossy, attractive personality than confused personality, positive personality than negative personality and others. Individual personality shows through operant behaviors and respondent behaviors vary from person to another as a result of the system those behaviors subject to. Noteworthy, personalities' differences is a result of behavior variation.

Personality can be known and its behaviors can be predicted through knowing the system which this character subjects to. This system is considered as a kind of obligation for personality.

Actually, we notice that this obligation is a religion, customs and traditions support each other and person always feels that they are connected with each others. Those obligations steam from our direct surrounding or the surrounding of this surrounding and so on.

Each conduct of those obligations meets the needs of person directly or indirectly. It holds and forming one sentence even if they appear to us isolated from each others, they will be integral part of this commitment.

(Bergson, 1971) says that commitment generally means the whole which owes to its parts, then grants each of those part the authority it enjoys. Hence, the whole work on strengthening the single and this appears when saying (This is a duty) when we hesitate about doing any duty. Indeed, we don't think frankly in a collection of partial commitments gather it to form full commitment. (p.15).

Behavior which forms the personality of the individual subjects to commitment. It may strength Individual not to break or bend this necessity but he still subject to it. To feel with this necessary even it was accompanied by a feeling of a capability to escape from it. This is also called commitment. Commitment is necessary for it doesn't come from outside completely. Everyone belongs to a community and to himself too. (Bergson, 1971) says that if the person goes deeply into himself, he will discover an authentic personality still increases and this authenticity increases as long as he goes deep through it. This personality can't be compared with others and can't be expressed.

If this is true, it is also true that we are connected with people, look like them and combine with them with a system that creates between us a correlation but is this the only way to connect with them? If there is, what is it?

Look at the aquatic plants that flow on the surface of water and stream shake them from time to time to find that their leaves convened upon water, give those plants endurance and stability while but the roots extended in the bottom support them to give them more endurance and stability.

Man's personality is also like those plants. Man's behaviors are subjected to system control which is commitment. This commit system socially backs up personality on surface (Community) at the point where its behaviors overlaps with other characters in this packed textile in behaviors which became social after this process. At this point, it becomes social. Hence, commitment connects all individuals. At the same time, there is a commitment inside personality itself that we find as another type of commitment and it is so strong to link this behavior with this personality.

Therefore, we find that commitment is a tie that connects all individuals of community. First, it is a tie connects person's behavior with his personality which organizes individuals' behavior in all various fields and sciences for community prosperity and leading individual towards his happiness. This makes ethics a science extends to all subjects and human behavioral practices and controls personality. Ethics is a science controls individual's behavior with himself, universe and its contents and his God. Every behavior or act of those acts has a moral pattern which individual should follow.

(At taloaa, 1995) mentions that complying with this pattern of behavior, which harmonizes with moral rule, achieves goodness and virtue as the trial to get out and deviate achieves vice. Therefore, we approximately can't find, in human behavior, what may deviate out of ethics field and frame. Therefore, today we find in ethics science what is called with political ethics, science ethics, medicine ethics, and economy ethics and ….etc. Any science does not established upon moral values and principles; we can't hope any good or benefit for man from it.

From this point, some psychologists confirm that behavioral problems and mental diseases from which some individuals suffer are resulted in moral problems from which those individuals suffer.

According to the aforementioned, we now can recognize the value of ethics in man's life. Commitment is a necessity which without it we can't live. In fact, man's personality does not go straight and doesn't achieve happiness and tranquility that are indicated through his behaviors but if he committed with high moral principles in all his acts and behaviors with himself and others for the tie that connects man with himself and others, is ethics.

(Chapter Two)

Professional Ethics

(Chapter Two)

Professional Ethics

1- Profession concept and synonymous.

2- Public function and employee concept.

3- Ethics and values.

4- Professional Ethics concept.

5- Functional behavior.

6- Resources of professional behavior ethics.

7- Moral formation of profession behavior.

8- Moral applications in functional systems in the Kingdom of Saudi Arabia.

1- <u>Profession concept and synonymous</u>:

- **Profession concept:**

Lexical meaning: work which needs to experience and skill (Al-Waseet lexicon, 2\1042).

Convention meaning: a set of works require certain skills performed by the individual through training practices. (Al Qussi, D.T) says that profession is a work occupied by the worker after receiving enough theoretical study and long- term practical training in scientific centers or specialized institutes and universities. Profession requires a set of skills, theoretical knowledge and rules that organize work inside the function, such as medicine, engineering and education.

- **Craft concept:**

Lexical meaning:: is derived from Professionalism which means earning (Al-Waseet lexicon, 1\167).

Convention meaning: is a work practiced by man who needs to short- term training.

(Al Qussi, D.T) defines craft as a manual and physical work practiced by craftsman in workshop, factory or in domestic service and others. It is not necessary to master this craft work through intensive theoretical study. It can be acquired through experience and watching repeatedly.

- **Function concept:**

Lexical meaning: what you got of work, food, money or others in a certain time. Moreover, it can be a certain service (Al-Waseet lexicon, 2\1042).

Convention meaning: unit of work consists of many activities combined with each others in essence and form and it may be performed by one or more employee.

Function is organizational entity including set of duties and responsibilities which commit their holder with certain obligations for having functional rights and advantages (Al Othaimeen, 1993).

- **Work concept:**

Lexical meaning: is profession and deliberate deed (Al-Waseet lexicon, 2\628).

Convention meaning: productive activity performed by man in function, craft or profession. Moreover, work is defined as profession, craft, pursuing and earning. Work is defined in (crown of the bride) book as a "work and profession" (Mimeni, 1994, p.28). Work in brief is effort exerted through his mind or any of his organs for a certain purpose. Moreover, work is also defined as a set of similar due functions which one person can perform when necessary. In the light of the foregoing, we can say that:

- **Every function is work, every craft is work and every profession is work.**
- **Consequently, profession means work and work refers to profession for work is defined as profession and the opposite.**

Professional Ethics

Ethics is considered as a true standard to describe a person of humanity and distinguish him from other creatures. It represents the beauty of man and the main core of sciences. Through ethics nations promotes and countries became stronger. It is the greatest mean to develop countries. If a country has employees work with honest and sincerity, it will have a great position between other countries. Therefore, we will discuss the concept of professional ethics and its importance.

1- Professional Ethics concept:

Ethics is defined as a set of values, costumes and traditions which the individuals of the society know to identify what is good, right and justice to organize their lives in community.

Profession is defined in brief as work that needs to experience and skill.

Profession is defined in details as a set of works requires specific skills performed by person through training practices.

Consequently, Professional Ethics has several definitions as follows:

- Science that deals with the duties which are imposed on a person according to his practice for a particular profession.
- Some people defined it as "Principles and standards which are considered as a base for the acceptable behavior for persons who practice the profession and undertake to commit it".
- (Al-Saud & Bettah, 1996) identified it as a set of assets and rules which employers follow them to maintain the quality levels of the profession and promote it.
- Professional Ethics: a set of guiding rules which control individuals' behavior when performing their professions.
- Work is defined as profession, craft, pursuing and earning.

Work is the activities performed by man whether they are industrial, professional, agricultural, commercial or...etc to achieve a certain aim. Therefore, profession means work and work refers to profession. Although there are some people see that every profession is a work but not vice versa for they think that profession requires mastery and accurate knowledge in contrary to work. Man may work in a profession he\ she does not master therefore, we cannot consider him\ her is a professional.

Based on the discussed above, we do not agree with this opinion because it defined work as a profession and vice versa. Moreover, any work man performs must be mastered because this is the Professional Ethics which disagrees with the previous point of view.

Consequently, Profession Ethics is a set of rules and principles which profession workers must commit with to maintain the quality level of their profession and promote it. It also called sometimes as "Work Ethics" or "Functional Ethics" which its essence is (Performing work without negligence). Some people define Professional Ethics as an application for the ethical principles through individual's behaviors in organizations. Consequently, values form the ethics of work of every individual and as a result, there will be an administrative behavioral pattern, which may be ethical or not, generated from those ethics.

(Iman and Mariam, 2011) defined Profession Ethics as a general set of beliefs, values and principles which control man's behavior when taking decisions and distinguishing between what is right and wrong, good or bad, lawful or unlawful and that the sources of those values and beliefs steam from family, friends, groups, formal curriculums, media and culture.

<u>We can extract as follows:</u>

Ethics is an evaluation and arranging test for our values which are in general ethical rules affect on behavior that is required by profession. Consequently,

Professional Ethics is Work Ethics which is Function Ethics that means:

Rules, principles, values and standards which are considered as the base of good workers' behavior and they must commit with.

"Functional Ethics" is an application for good values that an employee applies in his\ her behaviors at work. Those ethics are providing ethical and legal base for individual's behavior in various situations and circumstances which the employee face inside and outside his work. Ethics also reflects on laws, instructions, behavior rules and professional standards (Al-Ghamdi, 1430 A.H, P.5)

<u>2- Work Ethics and values:</u>

Ethics results in values that individual believe and adhere as it stated in several definitions of ethics.

Values are normative provisions that aim to determine behavior, acts and opinions of the individual, reflect his relation with his family, home and the world and form his scientific and intellectual tendencies. The denotations of those Values appear in what they reflect on their adopter of behavioral, knowledgeable and consciousness activities and the individual's positive or negative valuable dealings with people, things or situations.

(Akl, 2001) defined values as aims which individual seek to achieve them. According to this definition, values represent a reference for individuals to judge their behavioral patterns and to determine their aims in the various fields of life. Values are frankly expressed through phrases or implied through what the behavior of the individual as what said when defining values as" principles and standards which enable the individual to differentiate between true and wrong and what is desirable or not. (Al Othaimeen, 1993).

(Abdel Wahab, 2000) refers to M. Rokeach (American psychology scientist) definition of values as a firmly believe that acting in a certain way is better than acting in other available way or that pursuing a certain aim to live is better than pursuing any other available aim.

According to the above mentioned, we find that values represent normative provisions which adjust man's behavior and groups and determine what is desirable or not. Moreover, values represent certain aims which individual seek to achieve. Values as aims represent a reference determine the behaviors of the individual to achieve those aims.

Values represent the external ethical cover for each human activity as they work as a guideline for man's behavior and groups. Whereas the main index of values is behavior, values which individuals adopt at work are the determinants of their behavior. Consequently, values will affect the performance of work in the organization according to the importance role of values in affecting behavior and as a result on the performance of business organizations.

(Abdel Wahab, 2000) refers to the results of studies which are conducted in such field as follows:

1- Individual is guided by the value of personality to determine true and wrong behaviors therefore, changing of values is considered one of human behavior controls.

2- Recognizing that the differences in personal values of individuals help in interpreting the nature of disputes between those individuals in the organization. Furthermore, similarities in the personal values of the individuals help in interpreting the understanding between them.

3- The effectiveness of director's leadership role will increase when his values were similar to his employees' values and vice versa.

Therefore, we cannot deny the impact of values on individual's behaviors whether it is positive or negative, so here comes the role of leadership to stimulate good behavior and changing the negative individual tendencies as (Al-Sabagh, 1406 A.H) says that ethics of the public employee administrative behavior is one of the values outcomes that the employee believes in, prevail in community and transfer into the administrative authority through individuals and their dealings with each others.

Consequently, ethics elements and behavior patterns prevailing at work are derived from external environment. Moral or immoral behavior of the employee at work is an outcome of all prevailing values in society and naturally in the place of his work.

- **Values, ethics and behavior of individual in professional work relation:**

Values: believing in particular thoughts and beliefs and believing that they are a certain behavioral pattern and that it is the best one.

Ethics: the employee application for values which he\ she believe through a certain behavior in a certain situation in the organization.

Relation between them is:

Ethics is the practical side of values which are the belief side of ethics. In another word: values are the essence of ethics including belief and practice.

We confirm on the definition of (Iman and Mariam, 2012) who believe that work ethics are a set of values and rules which control the individual's behavior in business organization and the sources of those values and beliefs steam from family, friends, groups, curriculums, media and culture.

We can extract as follows:

Each individual in business organizations has ethics based on values which he\she believes in and then a kind of functional behavior will be generated. This behavior reflects people and community's vision for him\ her. Is this moral behavior or immoral? This vision varies from community to another according to the variation of values which people and community believe in it and have an effect on determining this behavior.

Ethical behavior of the individual in business organization steam from two systems of values:

System of values in community:

- Family values
- Group values
- Work values

Personal values system:

- Natural personal values
- Religious and doctrine beliefs
- Previous experience and educational level
- Health, psychological and physical condition

<u>**Importance of Professional Ethics:**</u>

Ethics has a highly importance in the life of human communities whatever those communities were. It is not just a factor of building civilization, it also represents a preservation of such civilizations to break-down and fall for nations' promotion achieves by ethics promotion and vice versa.

As individual's life will not be good without ethics and work, this work will not be good and fruitful without ethics to control its course for professional work needs a firm tie with ethics to have a positive reflection on its course and be fruitful in the various fields.

So, complying with ethics in professional work is necessary and a duty that every individual and business organization must adhere. Organizations will not only depend on the commitment of workers with professional ethics according to their personal beliefs, they need to commit with it as part of work requirements. Non compliance of professional ethics will negatively affect the performance of those organizations, so it must apply and follow ethics.

It's necessary in professional work to determine what the moral and immoral according to custom of those organizations to urge community to commit with. If this custom is absent, each worker in the organization will have his own standard which differs from person to another. Therefore, there must be firmly when dealing with such breach of those ethics for it is not possible to allow for each worker to act as he\ she likes. Moreover, it is not possible to deal with who does not respect profession ethics or underestimate it because this breach will make all workers behave the same. We can't accept the enmity to spread between workers. Consequently, profession ethics is administrative necessity. It is best for the organization to bind all workers to commit with these ethics according to regulation includes profession ethics according to the organization's vision. Moreover, there must to be deterring punishment to any worker violates it.

Although everyone should have profession ethics, the administration of the organization must set controls and producers to make workers commit with it. Some workers may believe in professional ethics while others do not unless by commitment with it.

(Ghamdy, 1430 A.H) referred to the aim of commitment with professional ethics as follows:

1- Controlling professional and personal ethics which each official in the state must have.

2- Understanding professional duties and reminding of positive and negative rewards system as a successful method to evade some forbidden behavior aspects.

3- Insuring balance between ethics provisions and the necessity to maintain the rights and freedom of employees.

4- Creating relations between the administration and citizen that based on mutual trust according to the purpose of the establishment of the utility.

5- Removing predominant characteristic that may organization's administration is described with.

6- Leadership that based on ethics and values has a big role in improving the performance and success of the organizations.

In addition, adhering professional ethics contributes in preparing and developing human resource to produce its works effectively because profession represents reference which worker's behavior subject to generally and in his work. The absence of the concept of positive work ethics is considered as an element affect negatively on human development which negatively reflects on the non ability of executing development programs in its economic, social and organizational sides.

Here are some reasons of the importance of ethics: improving business organization's performance, such as when there is trust between workers and administration, we find that it has a direct relation with the increase of labor's productivity. Employee who knows that organization's administration will appreciate his\ her efforts in short and long term, will perform his\ her work perfectly. When truth, Cooperation, respect and honesty are ethics that speared between workers, it will lead to encourage workers to work. Weakness of compliance with professional ethics and the absence of accounting will lead to corruption and deviation.

Moreover, the importance of profession ethics achieves as follows:

- Reminding professional worker with proper behavior that he\ she must comply with when performing profession.

- Creating desirable balance in the relations of professional workers practically.

- Urge worker to sense profession ethics and recognize it and be happy to apply the orders of Allah and conscience instructions.

- Professional Ethics not only organizes duties of profession worker towards clients but also towards his\ her colleagues, supervisor authority and society.

- Maintaining the relations of love between colleagues of the same profession, co-operation and mutual helping.

- Increases the production of worker which leads to the improvement of business organization's performance he\ she works in.

- Developing and promoting the community of the worker which leads to achieving civilization

Communities which developed their values and standards of professional ethics to form civilized cover for them through successive periods, such as Primitive communities and their firm ethical standards, industrial communities and their renewable and flexible ethical standards and finally knowledge international community and its relative ethical standards which includes this great evolution in economical, social, cultural, technological fields and others.

When we mediate our bright past as Muslims, we created this civilization through complying with Islamic ethics which our prophet Mohamed delivered us for his ethics was Quran. We were leading the world and when we abandoned our values and ethics, we became developing countries and no more leaders.

This means that, we promoted when our ethics promoted and vice versa.

Nations are strong with their morals * * * if these morals gone they gone

We can extract as follows:

Ethics improves the types of behavior and deeds. Those ethics is the outcome of values that are considered as human behavior determinants. Therefore, professional ethics is principles and standards that consider as basics of the behavior of the profession individuals that workers undertake to commit with. Whereas employees behavior is a set of rules which indicate for individuals how to act in situations they face with non compliance of Allah orders, their consciences or prevailing costumes in their community. Complying with those ethics improves workers' behavior which leads to the increase of their production and enhance the performance of the organizations the thing that creates development in society.

Professional Ethics that appears in professional and functional behavior of worker is a set of values which individuals of the community recognize and believe that they good, right and justice to organize their affairs at work.

How does professional ethics consisted in the employee's behaviors?

Undoubtedly, individual's behavior at work plays a great role that affect business organizations' performance. It is considered as cornerstone of environmental work behavior. (Al Moqsqs et la, 2011) mentioned that we need to explain individual's behavior that we deal with them to study and understand functional behavior to help in understanding and explaining everything occurs around us, especially in business organization's field to increase the need of employees, directors and colleges to understand each other for this understanding will be positively reflected on the performance of workers and benefits the organization and state. Therefore, it is important to analysis and diagnosis individual and group behavior in the place of work recognize all factors to achieve harmony between individual and organization he\she works for and determine factors that affect individual's behavior and organization effectiveness.

Behaviors and activities that individual perform at work, communication with others, reactions, satisfaction on work and performing his jobs. All those behavioral patterns represent the base of the performance of the organization and the individual's behavior affect with its personal characteristics which will not be right unless he\she commit with high ethical principles. Moreover, individual's behavior inside the organization affects with values. This behavior reflects on work environment.

Based on the foregoing, the importance and necessity of forming professional ethics in business organization appears.

Ethical formation of employee's behavior is necessary to explain what is the employee's behavior? What are the standards and basis of ethics which he\ she should to commit with? What are sources of those ethics and obstacles to commit with? What is the good mean to establish those ethics?

- **Functional Behavior**

Functional Behavior means "employee's behavior in the organization work according to his\her jobs, function, responsibilities and determinants of functional role. Functional behavior should to be appropriate for the requirements to achieve work jobs and the efficiency of achieving its aims" (Khatab, 1402 A.H)

Behavior is generally defined as "set of acts, deeds, changes and other activities which individual practices in his\ her environment to achieve his\ her needs and desires".

Several terms related to behaviors that commonly used in Labor and administration appeared. They include Functional Behavior, Organizational Behavior, Human Behavior, Administrative Behavior and other names refer to individual's behavior in business organization.

(Fetehy, 2005) explains that functional behavior is known as human and organizational behavior. It means" comprehensive trial to understand individual's behavior as an integral unit in the organization or the facility they work for whether they were individuals, small groups or all individuals in the organization as a comprehensive and integral units and the reaction of this facility with its external environment (Effects and political, economic, social, culture and civilized factors) with the behavior of employees who work for it (Individuals and their situations, emotions, motivations, efforts and abilities)".

(Al Yousef, 1431 A.H) Refers to administrative behavior as a set of various activities which individual shows inside the organizational environment, such as deeds, verbal, expressions and others by internal pressures as lack of incentives, non participation in making discussion, disregard of justice and equality between employees or external pressures like traffic and social and economic problems, So administrative behavior is originally human behavior but it is controlled or affected by systems and regulations which are due by the organization. Although there are various names that are interested in behavior inside organizations like administrative behavior, functional behavior and organizational behavior but those names are difficult to be separated because they are overlapped, coherent and almost have the same meaning even if there are various names.

Organizational Behavior is necessary at work for it is developing field for knowledge and includes a lot of important scientific principles which help in understanding people's behavior inside business organizations. Directors, colleagues and employees' need to understand each other because understanding affect work outcomes extremely and more understanding will lead to the increase of the organization performance. (Right understanding for individual's behavior at work enables organization or institution to deal with individuals in a right way and conduct the corrective behavioral procedures as required. Individual must commit with behaviors inside organization to promote his\ her work level and improve his\ her performance).

Consequently, concept of personality plays a great role at work filed and affects the professional employee behavior. A study of (Fetehy, 2005) confirms that personality affect the way which individual recognizes for his\ her work environment, evaluates and reacts with his\ her work for individual's behavior is an outcome of the continuous interaction between individual and situation. Personal characteristics affect various factors at work filed.

(Al-Moqasqs et la 2011) mentioned that functional behavior is just biological outcome inherited from mother, father and grandparents in addition to social factors like family, relationships with people in community, cultural factors steam from values, principals, costumes and religious factors represent in beliefs and religions. All those factors form his\ her character.

Individual, who seeks to achieve his\ her desire to have a certain position in the organization, looks to work as it eases or difficult achieving for his\ her desire. Then, he\she shows response and reaction differ according to his vision to work and his\ her contribution at work to achieve his\ her desires to have a high position.

Behaves and act in his\ her works according to his\ her vision and the extent of the contribution of labor to reach and achieve his\ her wishes in distinguished position.

Therefore, functional professional behavior is considered as important point for every administrative, practitioner and decisions maker which means that it is important for the individual, organization and state that seek development.

<u>We can extract as follows:</u>

- Administrative Behavior, Functional Behavior and Organizational Behavior are names difficult to be separated. Administrative Behavior is considered as a manifestation of human behavior which sometimes characterized with satisfaction and effectiveness. In another time, it characterized with non satisfaction and non effectiveness. So, establishing principle of discipline will be achieved by setting ethics generosities.

- Administrative Behavior is individual's behavior in his function. If his behavior improved, his production will increase and the performance of the organization.

- Administrative Behavior helps the employee to interpret, predict and control human behavior. Administrative Behavior, this part of knowledge which is interested in describing, predicting and controlling human behavior in his function whatever its position.

To be able to describe, control and improve this behavior in function, there must be a relation between administrative behavior and effectiveness of functional performance. In fact, this is what we noticed and confirmed by several studies including (Al wahab, 2009) that extracted to the existence of a positive relation between wise behavior and effective functional behavior whereas discovered that wise men excelled in performance.

Establishing rules for administrative behavior (Professional Ethics) would establish functional discipline, transparency, integrity, objectivity, qualification, allegiance and effectiveness principles in employee's behavior during performing their functional duties and jobs. Whereas professional ethics aims to direct employees to the necessity of providing fast and high quality services for clients (Community individuals) in Highest degree of professional.

There is no doubt that public function concept is necessary. Who is employee? What are his\ her mutual duties and rights? Consequently, employee recognizes and understands that behavioral rules steam from professional ethics and values of the society which employee must commit with to improve and adjust his\ her professional behavior.

Relation between values, ethics and individual's behavior in business organization:

Ethics is the profit of values because it is the application of values which worker believes in and this appears during his behavior in a certain situation. Therefore, we find out that behavior is the outcome or rustle of applying values which worker believes in.

The mentioned frame shows the relation between values, ethics and functional behavior:

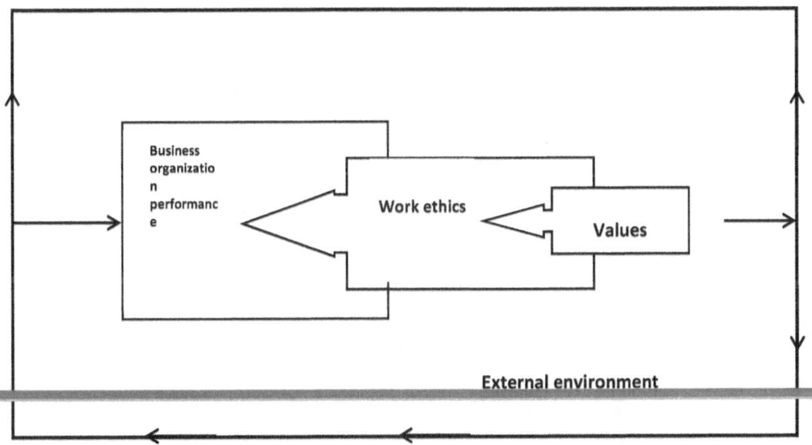

<u>*** Definition of public employee**</u>

There are a lot of concepts which determine the meaning of public employee, as like, as following:

- Every person service in public utilities managed by the state or by exploiting it directly and always holding an office in public management (Saadan; 2005).

- "Public employee" is the normal person that holding an office in one of public functions which subject to civil service system or one of the private functional systems as Cabinet System or Judicial System ...etc according to the requirements and qualifications of these functions.

* (Al-Yousef; 1431 A.H) defined the "Public employee" as: "Every person service in public utilities managed by the government or legal person under public law."

* Public employee in (Saadan; 2005) study as following:

- Every person employed by the administration under public law and contributes in public activity.

- Every person entrusted with a public function in the state for one of the three authorities functions whether such person was a governmental employee or otherwise against salary or against nothing.

*Also Public employee is defined as: "Every person or individual hold an office in a public function in the state performing the function duties against rights and privileges."

* (Gaafar; 1992) defined Public employee as: "The public employee is a tool of the state and people evaluate the state according to him\ her so that, Public employee must be qualified for this function to assure performing the functions' responsibilities perfectly.

* (Al-Nahaas; 2010) argued that work fields of the state became wide currently including public activity which no longer limited to an authority or judicial system. Public services can be classified as follows:

- Services related to the statehood (Defense- Security- Justice).

- Services related to achieving social stability (Social insurances and social welfare).

- Services related to organize living requirements (Commercial and civilian registration ...etc).

- Services related to good quality of life (Health, Education and Public Utilities).

Public employees provide service to people (I.e. they taking over a great responsibility in converting people ambitious and government targets into programs, goods and services) as they entrusted on the state and people security through their authorizes and specializations according to his\ her position.

Therefore, the employee role and his\ her good appreciation shall remain a basic factor in the frame of services provided to people which form is not be determined by laws, rules and plans whereas (Applicable laws which are not related to the employee moral obligation shall remain for review and notification, i.e. the employee morals and behavior effect seriously on the organization efficiency and thus the performance of the state).

We need a moral configuration of employees' functional behavior because ethics reflect the societal perception on human behavior. It is also classified any action as good or bad conduct according to the criteria or standards prevailing in this society.

Professional code of ethics' sources:

There is a set of ethical standards upon which the employee behavior to others is based and also determines his\ her normal relationship with them. The employee can only be committed to ethical standards of the group otherwise subjected to some kind of punishment. Usually, individuals are acting in the manner in which they find it consistent with the reference values of the group to which they belong especially if they considered that this action or behavior will lead to gain the group satisfaction and maintain its coherence.

The most important reasons that derive the employee to join the group are; the individual sense that laws and regulations governing the work of the organization provide adequate protection of his\ her right and in case the employee do not feel so, he\ she believes that belonging to a group to protect him\ her may fulfill that default in the relevant labor laws.

Accordingly, the most important sources of ethics as follows:

1. Religion

2. Soul and conscience control

3. Social environment

4. Leadership and ideal

5. Civil service laws and regulations

1. Religion:

The divine religions are considered the most important source of human morality which draws the individual actions, demeanor and methodology in life. The divine religions put behavioral morals and virtues reflected on the individual in his\her dealing with Allah, good treatment and correctness with all people because all persons are equal before the law. So that, religion is the most important source of the employee ethics but it is the main source of ethics in general.

Islamic sharia in the holey Qur'an and Sunnah of the Prophet Muhammad (PBUH) is the most important source for the responsible individual in all actions, behaviors and dealing with others (Managers or Subordinators), through dealing with external audience in the work or how to perform his\ her work in the required manner. Examples on morality related to work: intention, responsibility and penalty. These foundations are required by contemporary moral systems. Any researcher for the moral aspect in the divine religions will find two main approaches as follows:

1. Theoretical approach: establishes the theoretical foundations and rules in moral philosophy such as searching for human nature, Islam source, the responsibility and rules of human behavior.

2. Practical approach or work for behavior rules and virtues that enhance the society.

According to the foregoing; it is clear that faith is an important basic of ethics. Faith and ethical behavior are closely linked. For scientific basis of ethics; Islam determined an ethical framework for the individual according to its conception about the universe and the existing facts. Islam raises the Muslim worker on a mental education its purposes are related to science, knowledge and right values.

The most important ethics sources of Muslim employee in the Islamic Sharia:

1. Holy Quran:

The Holy Quran is the speech of Allah that revealed to his Prophet Muhammad (PBUH) that including all matters of religion and life. It is a code of ethics for Muslims in the whole life which is also Muslim constitution as a responsible person in his\her work. The Holy Quran is the speech of Allah (Is Exalted and Majestic) that expresses his willing so that, it is another source of direct and real ethical duty. The Holy Quran focused on essential and great matters that organize the behavior of individual and group in life, such as the following:

A. The true faith: the focus of a Muslim personality. According to the true faith and in the light of pure monotheism, Muslim behavior shall be straight without deviation and then he corrects his obvious behaviors.

B. General rules: Islam imposed general rules to organize Muslim life in treatments and so on. If these rules are followed, the individual behavior and treatments will get better because Islam is the way to deal based on compassion, intimacy, harmony, honesty, sincerity, honesty and peace between the individuals, groups and nations.

2. Sunnah:

It is the second source of the Muslim's ethics. Sunnah replete with the Prophet Muhammad (PBUH) deeds, words and dealing that presents the greatest examples of adherence with good characters. Allah said about the Prophet Muhammad (PBUH): {And indeed, you are of a great moral character} (Al-Qalam, 4). Malik reported: The Messenger of Allah, peace and blessings be upon him, said: {I have been sent to perfect good character.} A'isha "Umm al-Mu'minin (RA) said: {His character was the Qur'an} Source: Almusnad Aljamia, reported by Ahmed, 6\91. The Messenger of Allah (PBUH) is the greatest good example for Muslims as well as Sunnah is an important source for Muslim worker regardless his level in the work, whether in his functional obligations (professional) or dealing with others. We have found a reflection of moral commitment in the era of the Caliphs in their practical dealing (Al Othaimeen, 1993).

3. Companions morality:

Morality of the companions of the Messenger (PBUH) and his family are the third source for ethical commitment in the work. The companions gave the best examples in good morality when they applied their performance in all treatments in their works in managing the Islamic states which were at the golden age.

Elements of professional ethics pillars in Islam:

(Binding- Responsibility- Penalty)

* **Binding:** it is one of the most important elements which the ethical system in Islam is based on. Binding is the person's commitment with the whole humanity for being responsible for his deeds in this life, has honesty, message and freewill which controls his performance in the work, and the individual shall be accounted for his actions.

Therefore, ethical commitment supports professional ethics and one of its pillars. Commitment means: finding a specific behavior to be followed in the work so, this behavior must be clear and easy to be practically applied (Al-saadan, 2005).

Binding is connected with a power to order each person with the necessity felt by everyone whatever the current situation of feeling. It is also the necessity which makes the disobedience a real matter; therefore, a binding system of morality must be applied for workers which effects positively on the production and performance of business organizations. This binding System which is related to code of ethics is usually based on Islamic sharia.

(Draz, 1973) in his book argued that: How can we create an ethical rule without binding? Isn't it a conflict in limits? Or we kill conscience?" Binding is an essential rule which the whole ethical system is based on. Lack of binding may lead to miss the practical essence of wisdom, neglect responsibility failure to apply equitability, consequently chaos grow and system corruption.

Sources of ethical commitment in Islamic Sharia:

1. Religious revelation: religious guide man towards goodness and well-mannered, Allah the highest says: **{It is He who has sent among the unlettered a Messenger from themselves reciting to them His verses and purifying them and teaching them the Book and wisdom- although they were before in clear error.}** (Al-Jumu'ah, 2)

2. Mind: it is the light for man to go on the right, good manners and avoid vices. Quran has mentioned the actual proofs and reasons of a lot of warships and relations. Allah the highest says: **{O you who have believed, indeed, intoxicants, gambling, [Sacrificing on] stone alters [To other than Allah], and divining arrows are but defilement from the work of Satan, so avoid it that you may be successful (90). Satan only wants to cause between you animosity and hatred through intoxicants and gambling and to avert you from the remembrance of Allah and from prayer. So will you not desist? (91)}** (Al-Ma'idah, 90 & 91). Allah the highest says: **{Do you order righteousness of the people and forget yourselves while you recite the Scripture? Then will you not reason?}** (Al-Baqarah, 44)

3. Binding through intimidation and encouragement: Islamic ethical education the following:

Intimidation: Allah the Highest says: **{And [Remember] when your Lord proclaimed, 'If you are grateful, I will surely increase you [in favor]; but if you deny, indeed, My punishment is severe.}** (Ibrahim, 7)

Encouragement: Allah the Highest says: **{And if only the people of the cities had believed and feared Allah, We would have opened upon them blessings from the heaven and the**

earth; but they denied [the messengers], so We seized them for what they were earning.} (Al-A'raf, 96)

4. Binding on the power influence: there are people who need to the power influence which is the penalties imposed by the Islamic Sharia and the governor was authorized to apply them. Allah the Highest says: **{[Allah] will say, "Enter among nations which had passed on before you of jinn and mankind into the Fire." Every time a nation enters, it will curse its sister until, when they have all overtaken one another therein, the last of them will say about the first of them "Our Lord, these had misled us, so give them a double punishment of the Fire. He will say, "For each is double, but you do not know."}** (Al-Ma'idah, 38).

Gathering of all influences in Islam is to complete the means of binding for anyone devil pictured to him to get free from obedience and commitment. The source of binding in professional ethics in Islam is the feeling with Allah observation, while the source of binding in ethics theoretically is abstract conscience, feeling of duty or applicable laws.

*** Responsibility:** binding imposes responsibility which is followed by penalty. Bearing responsibility means that person is liable for his obligations, negative and positive decisions before Allah, his conscience and community. (Al-saadan, 2005) argued in his book that responsibility is the situation of a person who committed what requires accountability. The individual when committing any act that required accountability shall be intend to do so or not. Intention here means the person knows that what is being committed is considered to be a breach for there are set of ethics which cannot be ignored because it is identified by specific texts or gained by natural disposition. Muslim worker must feel responsibility when he\ she perform work and observe Allah. The Messenger urged people to bear responsibility when he said: **{All of you are shepherds and each of you is responsible for his flock. A man is the shepherd of the people of his house and he is responsible. A woman is the shepherd of the house of her husband and she is responsible. Each of you is a shepherd and each is responsible for his flock.}** (Sahih Al Bukhari, Friday's chapter, part 1, 893)

Responsibility is based on binding. If there is no binding, this will be determination of the outcomes of the ethics. If there is no binding, there will be no responsibility, consequently no equality and rights will be lost.

● **Remuneration: has three types as follows:**

1- Moral remuneration: it may be a reward or punishment. Reward to practice the moral rules is self-satisfaction which increases the infiltration of thought and the mastering of man's skills while practicing vice has its moral penalty too which is represented in enforcing the violated law which is repentance and setting right. In other words, setting right what is ruined by the worker at his work. This setting right has many forms:

- Incomplete work which shall be performed again properly sooner or later.
- A mistake shall be removed. This includes the right of Allah and requires Allah's forgiveness and the right of society (Mistake when doing such a work) and doesn't forgiven unless with liberating from those who are harmed.

2- Legal punishment: is related to his committing legal prohibitions. This is considered in itself as evil must be deterred and fixed, awakens peace and love spirit among people and maintained the basics of the human's life.

3- Divine remuneration: Quran refers to this remuneration in two forms:

First   : Promptly divine remuneration which will be in the world and has its material and moral sides.

Second: Divine remuneration in the hereafter. This will be in paradise for who obeyed or Hell for who deviated and followed his lust.

The employee should know that remuneration depends on the kind of his deed. Who performed work perfectly deserves reward represented in employee's due rights and who breached professional commitments deserves penalty according to the type of this breach.

This penalty may be a disciplinary one restricted in noticing, blaming, deducing from salary, disbarment the annual allowance and dismissal from service. Moreover, it also may be a criminal or disciplinary penalty. Penalty is the remuneration resulted from bearing responsibility. Furthermore, Reward is represented in having his functional rights with Allah's love, mercy and support.

- Allah the Highest says: **{And whoever fears Allah- He will make for him a way out} {And will provide for him from where he does not expect. And whoever relies upon Allah- then He is sufficient for him. Indeed, Allah will accomplish His purpose. Allah has already set for everything a [decreed] extent}** (At-Talaq, 2-3).

- Allah the Highest says: {**And whoever fears Allah- He will make for him of his matter ease**} (AT-Talaq, 4).

- Allah the highest says: {**Say, "O My servants who have believed, fear your Lord. For those who do good in this world is good, and the earth of Allah is spacious. Indeed, the patient will be given their reward without account."**} (AZ-Zumar, 10).

- Allah the Highest says: {**And if only the people of the cities had believed and feared Allah , We would have opened upon them blessings from the heaven and the earth; but they denied [the messengers], so We seized them for what they were earning**} (AL-A'raf, 96).

- Allah the Highest says: {**It is that of which Allah gives good tidings to His servants who believe and do righteous deeds. Say, [O Muhammad], "I do not ask you for this message any payment [but] only good will through kinship."And whoever commits a good deed- We will increase for him good therein. Indeed, Allah is Forgiving and Appreciative**} (Ash-Shura, 23).

- Allah the Highest says: {**And as for those who had believed and done righteous deeds, they will be in a garden [of Paradise], delighted**} (AR-Rum, 15).

Based on these related elements (The obligation is related to the responsibility and responsibility needs to remuneration to be achieved), the first resource upon which the employees depend is formed at different professional levels in the organization in their moral behavior. It is indicated that Muslim worker behavior in his\ her work is a message being delivered to its owners in sincerity and honesty. Allah trusted worker to perform work perfectly whatever his\ her professional level in the organization. The employee is a responsible whether works as a director (Leader), an ordinary worker, or an officer. And this is the moral behavior that helps the Muslim worker to achieve the organization aims, subsequently we finds that religion is the accurate resource of ethics even though what comes in the western philosophy schools.

Second: Self and conscience control:

Person doesn't seek to achieve any purpose except it has a return in his self so, (Fathy, 2005) argued that human must work in a comfortable and attractive job in order to advance it. This self will subject ethical rules to the worker perspective and appreciation. This is risky because it does not give ethical rules the necessary constancy, stability and continuity. Soul-searching is a step on the way to moral commitment of workers as it is a form of self-censorship applied by the individual on his\ her behavior (His\ her behavior in work). Soul-searching shall be more clear and effective for normal person but the abnormal is almost not committed to moral principles and values. Therefore the abnormal person does not judging him\ herself while the normal person faces sharp conflicts if he\ she tried a set of behaviors that conflict with ethical principles. Abnormal person consider breaching ethics as savvy or slyness by committing some behaviors such as follows: (Lying, theft, treason, bribery, deception and assault on the others' rights... etc) without being influenced or conscience suffering even if the others are affected significantly by these behaviors.

Soul-searching is usually based on the result of actions, commitment with religion and education methods in the surrounding social environment. Strong faith in Allah is closely linked with positive morals and vice versa. The surrounding environment may have a positive or negative effect on the individual moral which influence on soul-searching and conscience.

<u>Third: Social Environment</u>:

Social environment, which individual lives in and the crowd between the various sectors of society through customs, traditions, habits and values, is considered as one of the most important resources of variation that affects the worker's behaviors in business organizations whether in dealing with clients or with his colleges which affects his production and performance.

(Al Othaimeen, **1993**) confirms that we cannot ignore the role of social environment and what includes of customs, traditions and values that the worker acquires from family, school and the street he lives in for they all forms of resource of his behavior, acts and ethics at work.

(Al-Saadan, **2005**) mentioned that the worker transfers his inherited behavior to the organization. This behavior reflects the reality of his living environment and the circumstances of his financial life. The family that brings up her sons on the principles and religious ideals as, sincerity, honesty and respect, those sons will still hold tight on these principles to reflect their professional behaviors.

Moreover, educational institutions play an important role in preparing students to enter the functional field where it can direct, advice and teach them some affairs of ethics and public relations and their relation with our Islamic religious law. How our Islamic religious law mentioned this relation in the generosities of the ethics. How the individual adhere it to succeed in this world and hereafter.

Consequently, these institutions succeed in developing the positive behavior of the student toward responsibility, allegiance and sincerity in work.

Furthermore, the society in which harmonious political, social or dogmatic values, its individuals must transfer them to work and reflect on their behavioral practices during their work in the organization. If these values are based on Allah's law and the instructions of Allah's balanced religion, they will make sure to put an end for such ethical violations and punishes the violator and the mistaken one at work. In addition, they will not favor any one over another for his high rank or position in the society. Consequently, society affects the worker's behaviors positively or negatively according to it. The prevailing customs and traditions in the society have big effect in forming the ethical behaviors of the Muslim worker at his work because there is a close relation between the environment of ethics or the community and the development of work system in it.

Muslim worker, whatever his professional level, may expose some pressures from the society represented in his relatives, friends and family and their demanding to achieve their private interests and meet their desires. Sometimes this can happen through exceeding systems and instructions at the detriment of public interest. All business organizations usually establish ethical standards and values which worker must commit with such as, compliance with work, bearing responsibility and truth... etc. This may sometimes lead to the steam of a kind of conflict inside the worker about which one of these values should his behavior respond to at his work?

Worker's subjection to these pressures leads to the appearance of some immoral behaviors at work because of the absence of awareness, family's obligations and lack of breeding and ethical values in the soul of some individuals.

Therefore, (Abu'l-Hasan, 1996) says that society has main duty to help the employee to bear his public responsibilities through individuals and groups' conviction not to ask him for special treatment than others.

If community became sufficient, employee behavior will be sufficient. Consequently, service which is presented to community will be good.

Fourth: Ideal Leadership:

Leadership is considered as the main driver of work effectiveness because leader is the one who can use worker's behaviors and gather their energies to achieve the required aims.

(Al Shemiry, 2006) indicates that successful administrative leadership is the one that can spread the spirit of life in the organization by making every employee feels that he is a member in a group works to support him and his community to achieve the organization's aim. Ideal leadership is the one that deals with matters with firmness not with hardness, looseness or weakness. It will be moderate leadership that observes rights and duties, maintains man's indignity and complies with aim. Therefore, it can plant ethics excellence in the soul of the employees, guides the group spirit co-operated between each other, respects others and services the public interest.

Leader must treat all his employees in good faith, evaluates their performance according to efficiency and productivity without advocacy to another part, which achieves administrative justice in appointment and promotion, and is objective in awarding remunerations and incentives and distribution of works in justice and applies punishments upon violators without advocacy. Subsequently, ideal leader plays a role in affecting the behaviors of his employees at work through his behavior characteristics enable him to lead them for the improvement of their behavior at work and consequently, their performance and production.

Fifth: Legislations and Civil Service Systems:

Laws related to main resources direct workers' behavior in business organizations. One of the most important laws which represent a resource of ethical behavior of worker in business organizations is systems and legislations of civil service. Regulations, systems and laws issued by civil service departments and Labor Offices form a resource of ethics resources in the functional work. This can be achieved through ethical controls and laws that define individual's behavior and work motivate him to adhere with excellence ethics, promote with functional work and present good service for citizens (Al Othaimeen, 1993). Service administrations in various countries issue systems and regulations related to the employee's duties, behaviors, rights and how work is performed? Identifying and prescribing jobs. Public employee should comply with these instructions and laws as they are considered as a guarantee for ethical behavior which shall be committed with when performing work. Moreover, what are the forbidden acts that employee must not get close to them in function? Most of civil service systems tackled subjects related to ethics that employee should be characterized with such as, complying with official working hours, existing in workplaces to perform his functional tasks with high quality and allocating working hours to perform his tasks without delay. Moreover, they ban employee to accept any presents, reward, commission, and services whether directly or indirectly or bribery. Employee should also stop performing any activity leads to a real or apparent conflict between employee's personal interests and his functional tasks and responsibilities. Moreover, he should stop performing any activity leads to harm or damage the reputation of the governmental authority. Employee should maintain public fund and present service in transparency, justice, speed and tactfulness. Actually, the systems and regulations of work and civil service in the Kingdom of Saudi Arabia are distinguished more than other systems of the world because they are steam from Islamic religious law that rule the state.

The Kingdom of Saudi Arabia systems:

Labor and civil service system

There are other systems such as rule, cabinet and upper parliament systems and all of them work according to Islamic religious law.

- Governmental authorities issue labor functional systems:

- **Ministry of Civil Service**: It was named as Civil service commission and it issued labor system in 4 pages.

- **Ministry of Labor**: It is named for as Ministry of Labor and Social Affairs, then it separated to be independent with labor affairs only. It issued a system in 30 pages.

- **Ministry of Civil Service in civil service system**: This is related to public or governmental sector while Ministry and System of Labor related to private or non-governmental sector which is called organizations and companies.

Provisions of these two systems are:

- Ethical materials
- Obligatory materials
- Civil materials
- Disciplinary materials

- Governmental authorities that observe profession & professional ethics:

First: **Ministry of Civil Service** in which is related to the employees of the state. It is responsible for observing and accounting them. Regarding to private sector, **Ministry of Labor**, which issued the system, is responsible for it. As for the governmental authorities that observe the governmental sector, **Control & Investigation Board** observes the administrative affairs; **General Auditing Bureau** observes the financial affairs, and **National Society for Human Rights** (NSHR). It is a society established by the state to observe human rights and that no one is grieved whether he was an employee, worker or not. **Grievances Board** in the governmental sector and concerned with the **employee, Government** and **Ministry of Labor** whereas its judgment is required when some disputes arose between workers.

1- Ethics formation for profession behavior:

Standards related to ethical or social behavior is a responsibility symbolized in every employee as well as the organization itself. In addition, there are forces related to ethical decisions and contribute in making them. These forces are represented in the cultural textile, individual's ethics, organization's system and the external public.

These standards are the basic of employee's behavior formation. Moreover, the practice of professional ethics (Work) through the forces contributed in its formation is an integrated part to (Work, Management and Function). Therefore, ethics theory for (Samuel) assumes that administrative leaders have must focus on additional things other than benefits. This new idea regarding management asserts the need of taking administrative discussions related to ethical cretaceous and prevailing customs in the organization. (Samuel) also sees that ethics and competition cannot be separated from each other. He says, "We compete as a community and there is no community in anywhere will compete for a long time successfully with people who stab each others from behind" (Abd- Ellatief, **2006**)

Professional ethics are necessity for competing and producing to form ethics for profession behavior. The component elements of such ethics must be known.

(Abd- Ellatief, 2006) mentioned the most important component elements for work ethics in organization as follows:

1- Cultural textile and importance:

The appearance of such giant successful organizations with the leadership of their founders and what they have of cultural values were clear in their depth or products. Cultural textile is considered as a two-level building of notable characteristics and non notable ones. Notable characteristics represented in behavior, language and legends. Non notable characteristic represented in values, customs and common beliefs. Based on this description, cultural textile is a model for these two levels and directs the members of the organization (Employees) towards the solution of the problems related to its external adapt and internal balance.

Organizational culture represents one of the most important forces to form management ethics in the organization. It helps in composing the whole framework of values in the organization for personal values and ethical explanation transforms these values to acts which is an important phenomenon in making ethical decisions process in organizations.

2- Individual (Employee) Ethics:

Theories and practical principles do not affect the employee's behavior as we mentioned before. Values, customs and personality play very important role in directing behavior. Values are the base from which the individual's behavior forms. Therefore, the relation between values and ethics is deep and documented and through them behavior steams whether it was moral or immoral.

3- Organization System:

Policies, systems and a group of ethics principles, systems of award, testing and training are all one of the contributing forces in forming management ethics which can direct behavior towards a certain approach. Each system of the organization systems has a special effect on workers' behavior nature. In total, these effects generate force attract behavior and push it towards the approach that enhance or weaken the work through management ethics.

4- External Public:

Governmental systems, clients, beneficiary groups and market forces are all form the fourth force which contributes in forming management ethics and direct it towards a certain approach especially today's world which made the prescription of products during a period of time is un believable. These developments are combined with an increase of ethical scandals as a result of **Business Vision** which is based on profit and negligence of social responsibility. This paved the way to state's interfere and legislation of laws to protect the consumer and the interest of all parties.

Consequently, ethical formation for employee's behavior is based on many affairs of knowledge:

Knowing what is public function and employee's application for it must have behaviors related to him as an individual and an employee. Therefore, person or organization can form a strong ethics if these relations were powerful and positive which are the relation between values and behavior. The first element in ethical formation (Resources of Professional Ethics) using number of resources to identify what the wrong and right, for example religious resource (Qur'an, Sunnah, Companions' Ethics) conscience, social environment, ideal leadership, systems and laws ... etc.

These resources must lead its beliefs and conventions to what is right or wrong. As we mentioned before, elements of professional ethics are based on values and these resources. Therefore, employees (Workers) should not be interested in all what is proper and useful for them. These resources must lead them to what is wrong and right. Employee's ethical behavior consists from a several components sneaking in him\ her soul and the effect exchanges a combine of values and beliefs which grant him\ her a personality to judge on what is right and wrong about certain situation and a certain case.

8- Ethical applications on professional functional systems in the Kingdom of Saudi Arabia:

Introduction:

Function in the Kingdom of Saudi Arabia is Governmental or Non-Governmental. Governmental function is controlled by the Civil Service System issued by civil service board decision No. (1) on 27\07\1397 A.H. Office of the Chairman of the Council of Ministers approved it by letter No. (18562) On 20\07\1397 A.H

You can see it in the website of Ministry of Civil Service: http:\\www.mcs.gov.sa

Non-Governmental function is controlled by labor and work system issued by the approval of cabinet No. (745) on 23,24\8\1389 A.H and the royal decree No. (m\2) on 06\09\1398 A.H.

You can see it in the website of Ministry of Civil Service: http:\\www.mcs.gov.sa

First chapter: Professional Ethics in the Civil Service System:

The Civil service system talked about some aspects of professional ethics related to the terms of designation, employee's qualifications, keeping, complying with office hours, treated some negative Ethics such as bribery and abuse of office, indicated employee's rights, duties and penal sanctions in case of deliberate violation.

It is noted that these regulatory aspects consist with the teachings of Islam as what is referred to before. Therefore, commitment with these systems is considered as compliance with Islamic religious law and functional one. The employee shall be appointed on applying the regulations where he\ she can sense the wage from God because it is obedience to God Almighty and the governors, and achieve to community benefits.

First Research: Ethical Materials:

* **First Article: Efficiency**: Professional ethics requires that employee must be qualified to bear responsibility of function as the Prophet-PBUH- says: {**When the government is entrusted to the undeserving people, then wait for the Last Day**} (Sahih Al-Bukhari\ Knowledge Virtues-59, by Abu Huraira**) government is entrusted to the undeserving people** means appointing unqualified persons. Therefore, Prophet –PBUH- {**appoints qualified persons as he appointed** Abd-Allah ibn Umm-Maktum **to be Imam in prayer**} (Narrated by Diya in al-Mukhtārah, Isnad

Hassan (Good) (7\91) by Anas: **{Prophet–PBUH- appointed Ibn Umm-Maktum as a governor of Medina (in his absence) twice while he was blind}**. Moreover, Prophet–PBUH- **{appointed Zayd ibn Harithah}** (Narrated by Al-Bukhari (El- Mghaze\ Battle of Mu'tah- 4013) **{then the Prophet appointed Zayd's son Usama to lead the army}** (Narrated by Al-Bukhari\ Prophet Mission Usama bin Zayd- 4198). **{Next the Prophet appointed Bilal to call for prayer}** (Narrated by Al-Bukhari (adhan\ Starting adhan - 579).

Article No. (1) Of Civil Service System entitled "Efficiency" stated:

Efficiency or competence is the basis for the selection of personnel to fill public office. Competence is the sum of the elements of self recipes in a person related to the efficient technical and administrative competencies and attendance, good behavior and other elements left to the discretion of administration.

Moreover, it stated in Article No. (4) Of The Civil Service System in terms of designation to be an employee:

- Good conduct.
- No doomed legit or imprisonment in involving moral turpitude or dishonesty offense until three years at least after imprisonment or applying the legit.
- Not dismissed from service of the state for disciplinary reasons unless he has been at least three years of the issuance of this decision.

To confirm this term, the Logan of Ministry of Civil Service as Allah the Highest says: **{The best one you can hire is the strong and the trustworthy.}** (AL-QASAS, 26).

***Second Article: Compliance with working time:** honesty requires that employee must maintain the time of his function, not to waste it and that function negligence is forbidden for it is considered as cheating and taking the money of the state by falsehood. The Civil Service System confirmed in its article No.(11) as follows: employee shall allocate working time to perform his job duties.

This commitment means that who does not comply with this duty will be exposed to be punished.

*** Third Article: Maintaining secrets**: forms and elements of function honesty is to maintain secrets. The Civil Service System asserted in its article No. (12), clause (E) included: employee shall not disclose secrets he saw according to his job. Employee shall comply with this duty whether he is still working or after leaving the service. "Functional Secrets" means such information or data that are seen according to his job and these secrets may remain hidden from the outsiders.

Fourth Article: Good treatment with the reviewers: it is considered as one of the elements of professional ethics agreed on and there are evidences confirm it in Quran and Sunnah. The Civil Service System asserted in its article No. (11) as follows: employee shall take into account the special ethics of tact in his actions with public, his superiors, colleges and subordinates. These manners exist in Islam and sometimes are called as "Decency" whereas Islamic ethics include smile, saying a good word, respect the eldest, having mercy...etc.

Moreover, it asserted in its article No.(12), clause No.(1) having mercy with reviewers which is good ethics: employee shall be kind with shareholders related to his work and perform the required facilitates to them and transactions within the competence of the system boundary.

Fifth Article: Not to exploit position: honesty and integrity of the employee also includes not it exploits his position for personal interests. The Civil Service System in its article No. (12), clause (A, B): it prohibits employee to misuse of functional power and influence peddling.

Sixth Article: Maintaining Virtues: If the Civil Service System conditioned good conduct to appoint employees, employee must keep his Islamic moral and behavior during his work and outside it. Article No. (11), clause (A): employee must rise above all what tuft position the honor and dignity, whether it's at work or outside.

Muslim employee should practice Islamic moral in his life and shall be subject to the obligation to no harm to the reputation of this post or distorted by any nature. This concept is wide and includes staying away from: alcohol drinks, deception, deceit, forgery, meanness.

Seventh Article: Obedience to Officials: Referring to the terms of work is to be legal. Based on this, employee has been ordered in Quran where Allah the Highest says: **{O you who have believed, obey Allah and obey the Messenger and those in authority among you}** and the Prophet-PBUH- says: **{obeying to those that Allah has put in authority over you}** (Sahih El-Gamaa (12), by Abu Huraira May Allah be pleased with him). The Civil Service System asserted in its article No. (11), clause (C) this following principle: employee must implement orders issued to him accurately, honestly and within the limits of the secretariat of the regulations and instructions.

Eighth Article: Accounting Personnel: one of the above mentioned elements of Professional Ethics is "Accounting Personnel" to ensure integrity and discipline in performing work. The Civil Service System asserted in its article No. (36) this subject: Periodic reports on each employee according to a list issued by the Head of Civil Service Board (Applicable regulation is "List of functionality" published in 1404 A.H).

I said: in order to make sure that these reports reflect employee's integrity, they must be integrity and do not favor any employee for personal interests or other effects.

Second chapter: professional ethics in Labor Law:

Labor Law is concerned with organizing Non-Governmental functions which are important as government functions because large numbers of citizens work in private sector for it contributes in maintaining the stability of national economy.

Labor Law talked about some aspects of professional ethics such as justice, good treatment, non working in forbidden things, fulfillment of contract, maintaining secrets, harmlessness and having mercy. It is important that Labor Law is concerned with establishing professional ethics because the increase of such ethics in private professions will abolish crime, deceive and injustice. Its reflection will be through the increase of financial income and moral development of society.

First research: Ethical Materials:

*** First Article: legitimacy of work:** Labor Law conditioned that the company's activity must be legal and asserted in its article No. (94) of the forth chapter that: employers must tighten surveillance to not allow entrance of any forbidden materials into workplaces. If anyone possesses these materials or use them, will expose himself\ herself to deterrent administrative penalties in addition to the legitimacy ones.

This consists with profession's provisions in Islam which is mentioned before. If the existence of forbidden materials is banned in workplaces, it is more appropriate that if the company or the organization's activity is forbidden or illegal, penalty must be consist of the legitimacy penalty and the administrative one.

*** Second Article: Good Behavior:** this includes many elements combine good treatment and commitment with public virtues which is an important part of professional ethics. Labor Law conditioned in its article No. (96) of the forth chapter as follows: workers shall be comply with good behavior and ethics during work.

If worker violated Islamic behavior, employer may terminate the contract without reward in accordance with article No. (83) of the forth chapter: employer may not terminate the contract without reward unless in the following conditions: if it is proved that employee has bad behavior or commits an act violates of honor or honesty.

As compliance of good behavior is a duty on the worker, it is also a duty on the employer in accordance with article No. (91) of the forth chapter: the employer shall treat his workers with proper respect and abstained from any say or act hurt their dignity or their religion.

Good behavior means that the employer should be kind with workers. He may not hire teenagers, minors and women in dangerous works or harmful industries such as machines in case of its operation with energy, mines, stone quarries and the like as was stated in the article No. (160) of the tenth chapter.

Moreover, company or organization shall allocate break time during office hour and pray time. Moreover, it also shall allocate office hours in a way that does not exhaust the workers in accordance with the ninth chapter (9).

If the worker was exposed to bad behavior from the employer, he has the right to leave work without notice as it was stated in article No. (84) of the pervious chapter: worker may leave work before the end of the contract without prior notice in the following conditions:

If the employer or who represents him attacked or committed an act violates ethics or virtues towards the worker or any his family members.

Moreover, worker may leave work if he was exposed to deliberate harm according to article No. (84): worker may leave work before the end of the contract without prior notice in such conditions: if there is a grave danger threatens the worker's safety or his health and the employer knew this danger and did not take any action to remove it.

All the above mentioned asserts the commitment with good behavior and Islamic moral with workers, be kind with them and treat them with the proper human treatment.

*** Third Article: Fulfillment of contract:** Islam obliges the contractors to fulfillment the legal contract as it was mentioned before. Labor Law prevents hiring the worker in a work other than the agreed one in the contract as it was stated in article No. (79) of the previous chapter: worker shall not be charged with work that is essentially differs from the agreed one unless with a written consent by him; or in the necessary status or may be; what the work nature requires for temporary time.

In the case of breaching of each party with what is agreed with the other party, the last one has the right to terminate the contract as it was stated in article No. (83): employer shall not terminate the contract without a reward unless in certain conditions as follows: if the worker does not perform his essential duties included in the work contract.

Worker also, shall leave work before the end of the contract term without prior notice in certain conditions as follows: if employer did not fulfill his commitments towards the worker and if the employer charged the worker with a work which is essentially differs from the nature of work included in the contract as it was stated in article No. (84).

* **Fourth Article: Honesty:** Labor Law stated on the necessity of workers to be honest and trusted on the materials and properties of the company or the organization at their disposal as it was stated in article No. (96) of the fourth chapter: workers shall return the unused materials to the employer and preserve the machines and tools at their disposal .

Maintaining secrets is a form of honesty: workers should maintain work secrets as was stated in article No. (96) of the fourth chapter: workers shall maintain the technical, commercial or the industrial secrets of the products they produce or contributed directly or indirectly in producing them. Generally, all professional secrets related to work and disclosing them may cause harm to employer.

If worker discloses work secrets, employer shall dismiss him without any notice as it was stated in article No. (83) of the fourth chapter: employer shall not terminate the contract without a reward, prior notice or compensate the worker unless in certain conditions as follows: if it is proved that worker disclosed industrial or commercial secrets related to his work.

* **Fifth Article: Justice**: The Kingdom of Saudi Arabia established Labor office in each area to bring justice between workers and employers and settle their disputes according to law as it was stated in article No. (75) of the fourth chapter: worker who is dismissed from work without reasonable cause, has the right to demanded with cancelling this dismissal and submits the request to the director of the labor office.

It is fair that the worker has the right to complain when he was cheated by the employer in accordance with article No. (84) of the previous chapter: worker has the right to leave work before the end of the contract term without prior notice in certain conditions as follows: if the employer or who represents him cheated the worker in the time of contracting related to work terms and conditions.

Employer shall terminate the contract if the worker fabricated to get the work in accordance with article No. (83) of the previous chapter: employer shall not terminate the contract without reward unless in certain conditions as follows: it is proved that the worker fabricated in order to get the work.

*** Sixth Article: Sex Segregation**: it is mentioned before that profession conditions require separation between men and women in workplaces in accordance with article No. (160) of the tenth chapter of Labor Law: men's working with women at the same work place and in any utilities or other places is not permitted in any case.

We can abstract as follows:

- To constitute ethics and behaviors, we must completely know what is function? What are his duties towards function? Who is the employee? How do ethics and values affect his functional behavior? Moreover, employee's behaviors affect with the resources of work ethics to result professional behavior.

- Allah the Highest says: **{Say, "Indeed, I am on clear evidence from my Lord, and you have denied it. I do not have that for which you are impatient. The decision is only for Allah. He relates the truth, and He is the best of deciders}** (AL-AN'AM, 57)

- Allah the Highest says: **{You worship not besides Him except [mere] names you have named them, you and your fathers, for which Allah has sent down no authority. Legislation is not but for Allah. He has commanded that you worship not except Him. That is the correct religion, but most of the people do not know}** (YUSUF, 40).

- Allah the Highest says: **{Then they His servants are returned to Allah, their true Lord. Unquestionably, His is the judgment, and He is the swiftest of accountants}** (AL-AN'AM, 62).

- Allah the Highest says: **{Say, [O Muhammad], "Sufficient is Allah as Witness between me and you, and [the witness of] whoever has knowledge of the Scripture}** (Ar-Ra'd,43).

- **Resources of Professional Behavior Ethics**: most important of these resources is the religious resource from which individual derives from all of his acts and behaviors whereas religion plays an important role in constituting individual's thought and conscience which has great effect in their ethics generally and then in the scope of function.

(Al-Gendy, 2008) indicates that the main aim of the Islamic method of administration is to establish an authority to achieve the unity of team at work, the co-operation of its individuals and working on creating social environment can provide as possible a spiritual and material life for its individuals in the manner drew by Islam. Furthermore, "Ethical Values" refers to the functional community in Islam based on this comprehensive rule as Allah the Highest says: **{You are the best nation produced [as an example] for mankind. You enjoin what is right and forbid what is wrong and believe in Allah. If only the People** of the Scripture had believed, it would have been better for them. Among them are believers, but most of them are defiantly disobedient} (ALI 'IMRAN, 110). According to this rule, human and social relations are organized at work in a way that brings happiness to workers and increases their productivity. It also indicates that whatever people have of knowledge, progress or prosperity the will be always slaves of Allah and need to Allah's legislation which falsehood can never approach it and there will be no happiness unless by following it. Development of the organization performance should include the coordination of efforts aimed to improve the level of workers' life through providing opportunities to form good relations among them based on nobility, sublimation, power of faith, good morals and co-operation.

"Self" conscience control is considered as a resource of noble rules established to incite workers to practice this control not as they are afraid from someone or they desire in power or position but in order to account himself. To observe his behaviors and treatment with others especially if this "Self" believes in Allah, it will find that this control is effective because it only fears Allah and desires its mercy. Workers will perform work and feel that Allah, who knows everything, observes them.

- Moreover, social environment and ideal leadership is considered as a resource of employee's ethical behavior as well as Civil Service systems and legislations issued in various states, instructions and regulations related to the rights and duties of the employee which oblige him to commit with these systems and legislations.

Public employee is now has Professional Ethics. He has certain rights and guarantees and in return he subject for specific commitments. These commitments include duties that require performing perfectly by the employee and forbidding acts which shall be stopped according to this responsibility. These commitments, which issued by systems and legislations of Civil Service in the states, are from the resources of professional behaviors.

However, there are reasons and factors may lead the employer to deviation of his function commitments and duties. We will discuss Administrative Corruption and Deviation of employee behavior.

<u>Main values based on Professional Ethics in Public Utilities and Administrative Authorities:</u>

Defining and identifying of the main values which public utility based on is considered as accurate process. In Europe, it has been noticed that the value of (Non–alignment) is the main value and the best mentioned as it provides equality before the law and administrative organization. All these values according to the European arrangement as follows:

- Non–alignment.

- Legitimacy.

- Integrity.

- Transparency.

- Usefulness (performance which leads to the required result).

- Equality.

- Responsibility.

- Justice (Iman & Mariam, 2012).

Many writers and researchers referred to the elements of the public function ethics as follows:

1- Commitment with systems and laws.

2- Respect of the values and customs of the society.

3- Justice and Non–alignment.

4- Respect of time and noncompliance with office hours.

5- Loyalty and allegiance to the organization.

6- Work affection.

7- Honesty, integrity, wisdom and sincerity.

8- Speed and mastering when accomplishing work.

9- Maintaining state or company properties.

10- Developing the scientific and practical efficiencies by the directors (Hagy, Al Sawaf, D.T).

Chapter Three

Administrative Corruption

&

Deviation of employee behavior

Administrative Corruption

&

Deviation of employee behavior

1- Administrative Corruption definition and functional deviation

2- Its standards

3- Its forms

4- Its reasons, impacts and methods of solving

Administrative Corruption & Deviation of Employee Behavior

Ethics reflects community's vision to human behavior as well as it classifies any good or bad behavior according to prevailing standards in society and all ethical values related to the vision of individuals and groups towards improper behavior. Ethical problems are found in public services wherever employees are, who abuse their positions in somehow that expose or may expose public trust to danger because of values opposition or as a result for the trial of achieving some forms of personal interests to the detriment of public interest, and whether they were jointly or separately.

Therefore, administrative corruption is considered as one of the negative phenomena in all human societies because this kind of work is based on man who performs a job and his thought, work and money affects the society. This man naturally composed of a collection of instincts, tendencies, cretaceous, lust and requirements. Consequently, administrative corruption is found in all societies and is considered as terminal illness and obstacle for the progress of these societies.

Administrative Corruption & Deviation of Employee Behavior Definition:

In language: Corruption is against righteousness.

Some writers distinguish between the terms of "Administrative Corruption" and "Functional Deviation":

(Abu'l-Hasan, 1996) thinks that "Administrative Corruption" is that kind resulting from bad faith, intentionally and with malice aforethought; this type is the most dangerous one.

As for "Functional Deviation", is resulting from the negligence of the responsible employee, inefficiency, disinterest and administrative carelessness or mismanagement.

Surely, this represents a breach of the employee when performs his\ her duties and must be punished for it but it is less dangerous and can be treated. On the other hand, "Functional Deviation" is not a match for "Administrative Corruption" but it will be eventually unless it is treated. Many writers and researchers did not distinguish between corruption and deviation and referred to them as the same.

(Al-Kodah, 2003) explains that there can be distinguish between the concept of "Administrative Corruption", the concept of "Administrative Error" and the concept of "Legislative Corruption".

- **Administrative Error:** The act which includes unintentional breach committed by the administrative. This concept has been distinguished by the addition of the word "Intention" to the word "Breach".

- **Legislative corruption:** Resulting from the issue of laws and systems which conflict with Islamic religious laws in text or in intention. Therefore, there is a condition in the definition which that the authority that has the breach must be legal to be able to say that it contains "Administrative Corruption".

In this book we assert that administrative corruption, functional deviation, administrative error and legislative corruption are many pictures for administrative corruption which are immoral behaviors.

There are many researchers tried to identify the concept of "Administrative Corruption" as follows:

- (Iman & Mariem, **2012**) defined "Administrative Corruption" as a breach of the honor of the job and the values and beliefs which the employee performs. Moreover, it can be the abuse or misuse of public function for personal interest. This is happening when the employee request a bribery for conducting certain services which he\ she supposed to perform it as being responsible for this position.

- (Ronald Reth, R Waribh, Edgar Sembkens, E. Simpkins) defined the concert of "Administrative Corruption" as any act or deed is considered as corrupted if the society judged as so and the one who commits it felt guilty. (Fahla, 1992)

- An American dictionary of social sciences defined the concept of "Administrative Corruption" as an abuse of power to gain a benefit or a profit for an individual, group or a class through violating law or breaking the high ethical behavior standards. (Could J & Kolb, 1964, P: 142).

- Moreover, "Administrative Corruption" is defined as a misuse of official authority to achieve personal benefits for the employee or one of his\ her followers through breaking laws, systems or high ethical standards (Zain, 1996).

- (Al Shemiry, 2006) defined "Administrative Corruption" as every behavior result from a violation of values an standards which control the society whether they were known or un-known. Devotion act results from the harm of others and their private and public prosperities.

- (Al Othaimeen, 1993) defined "Administrative Deviation" as employee's misuse of power for a personal aim other than public interest as a personal benefit, favoritism or to revenge from his\ her rivals. Deviation is one of bad ethical behavior of the employee which dishonors the dignity of public function.

There are many standards used by researchers concern in this study. "Administrative Corruption" can be abstracted as follows:

<u>**First: public opinion standard**</u>:

This standard is relatively new. Supporters of this standard divided "Administrative Corruption" into three types and each type has a color.

1- **Black Administrative corruption:** The behavior that all people and workers agree that it is Lousy and bad and who commits it must be convicted and punished.

2- **White Administrative corruption**: The behavior that all people and workers bypass it and do not tend to punish who commits it (People and workers accept a certain behavior).

3- **Grey Administrative corruption:** It is in-between the two mentioned types. This happens in the cases when certain members of the society ask for the conviction of the one who commits it while public opinion in-between.

(Abd- Ellatief, 2006) says that this means when managers consider that an employee did something bad and as a result led to a certain success or failure, it acquires black or white color. If this behavior or act were not accepted or rejected completely, it will acquire grey color.

<u>**Second: Corruption Practitioners' Standard (Interest standard):**</u>

According to this standard, "Administrative corruption" can be individually or organizational for it represented in activities and deviated behaviors which individual practice to achieve personal interests. Organizational corruption represented in deviated activities which are practiced by a corrupted system\s and they are usually including group of individuals that all or some of them may be from the administrative authorities concerned with the practice of administrative corruption and others outside these authorities but they all connected together with certain personal interests from outside entities.

(Al-Kodah, 2003) says that the purpose of approving such standard because the consideration of administrative corruption as advancing of private interest over the public one by someone who is officially appointed to maintain public interest. It also means the misuse of public function, power or resources to achieve private interests.

<u>**Third: Legal Standard (legislative):**</u>

This standard is preferred by legal researches because they restricted administrative corruption in breaching laws, systems and instructions which must be functionally compliance and usually associated with seeking personal interest.

Corruption appears as a deviate behavior of the official duties for a public function because of finance benefits or special position. It also is a behavior violates law through practicing the types of behavior that advance private interest.

For example, illicit gain through the public function, spread of nepotism and bribery, , embezzlement, functional negligence, disinterest at work, wasting time, spread of functional hypocrisy, suspicion and doubt relationships, mistrust between directors and employees, absence of responsibility and self commitment and conflict for power.

Fourth: Value Standard:

The approval of this standard means that corruption is a form of deviation from the prevailing values in society which considers these values must be committed with within the functional frame. This deviation is usually occurs for achieving personal interest or the like.

This means that corruption is a moral crisis in behavior reflecting a breach in values and deviation in directions as well as the level of controls and standards which are recognized to be a custom or legislation in the life of the group and constituted the value component in public function (Al-Kodah, 2003, P.8). Administrative corruption is not by necessary to be a deviation from the prevailing values in society. It can steam from committing with these values which differ from the patterns of proper behavior.

Fifth: Immoral Behavior Standards (corruption) described by (Dui Vidi):

(Dui Vidi, 1981) explained the standards of immoral behavior by hypothesis that immoral behavior includes all acts that not allowed by laws or unwanted acts as the abuse of public resources (Including the abuse of authority for personal interest). The scope of immoral behavior may include the following features:

(a) Activities that breach the legal regulations of the state and who commit them will be subject to legal prosecution.

(b) Activities that conflict with the main principles of ethics (Even if society does not practice them).

(c) Activities that are practiced for hidden or subtle pressures whether they are unconsciously or not or by the motivation of loyalty, allegiance, kinship, friendship and advocacy for social, political or religious class or bigotry for a certain gender. Consequently, immoral behavior is not only restricted in the activities forbidden by law as bribery and wasting money but extends to include other activities as nepotism, favoritism of relatives and friends, abusing authority by abusing the official position, disclosure of information and governmental secrets and joining a forbidden political activity.

<u>Immoral behavior types (Administrative Corruption and Deviation):</u>

Some acts in a certain community are considered as acts who commit them must be blamed and scolded while in other community these acts do not have the same consideration. Consequently, preparing a list includes all types of immoral behavior is considered as a difficult task and maybe dangerously misleading. Thus, the following types of activities are generally considered as an immoral behavior in many states:

(a) Bribery, embezzlement, forgery, illicit gain, nepotism (Patronage), favoritism of kinship and abuse of power.

(b) Conflict of interests: activities which targeting the achievement of personal interest as combining between a governmental function and other external works and misuse of public funds.

(c) Misuse of authority such as, misuse of official secrets and information to achieve benefit for a private organization, favoritism of kinship and friends by awarding them licenses, bids, loans or subsidies, blackmailing or accepting gifts and gratuities without any right. Moreover, the usage of public funds for personal interests such as, using the cars of the organization he\ she working for, printers, phones or the like of the properties of this organization. You find the employee uses these sincerities and abuse them for his\ her interests.

(d) Hiding the aspects of default and protecting it.

(e) Breaching systems and instructions such as, disrespect of working time, the employee's abstention from performing the required work or disrespect of work itself by refusing the work awarded to him or performing the work carelessly.

(e) Inactivity and laziness, noncompliance with directors' orders and instructions and breaching the dignity of function by committing indecent act by the employee as using drugs and alcohol drinks or involved in honor crimes.

<u>Immoral Behavior Reasons (Corruption) and its Impacts:</u>

Based on the foregoing, there is a necessity of highlighting the reasons and impacts of immoral behavior in society and these reasons are divided into four groups as follows:

1- Weakness of religious motivation in the workers' soul.

2- Political reasons.

3- Socioeconomically reasons.

4- Administrative reasons.

5- Urban reasons.

6- Structural reasons.

We will discuss these four groups as follows:

1- Weakness of Religious Motivation in The Workers' Soul:

Noncompliance with the main principles and rules when practicing work and not sensing Allah's observation is one of the important reasons of administrative corruption and the deviation of individual's behavior from the proper behavior inside and outside the organization.

In addition, there are some workers who restrict religiousness and complying with Islam rules and principles on certain fields do not exceed devotional rites which makes the employee excludes from religiousness (Complying with Islamic principles) his relation with people (Who work with him in the organization or clients outside the organization) inside the organization. In addition, this worker does not follow these religious principals in his administrative practices which are considered as the most deviation of worker's behavior, the organization and the state.

2- Political Reasons:

Employee performs his\ her work in the administrative authority of the state during the current political situations. Consequently, his behavior's pattern whether it was moral or not will be affected according to the nature and characteristics of this political environment. It is also noticeable that the employee's policy towards the governed political regime whether it was for fear or respect depends on the nature and the characteristics of this political regime. Thus, the employee's behavior will be affected according to his recognition of the effectiveness of the imposed observation by the governmental and legislative authorities. Regular observation on the administrative authority achieves the process of revision and evaluation of the performance and behavior of workers. (Dui Vidi, 1981) thinks that when the legislative authority becomes incapable as a result of the dictatorship and power of the president of the state or any other reasons, the responsibility of the employee will mostly subject to the desires of dictator CEO. Moreover, the integrity of the judicial authorities and the degree of independence of the executive authority affect the employee's behavior.

Whenever the employees feel that they can get away with their legal and constitutional violations, certainly there will be more of these immoral acts and behaviors. Those employees may even try to defend their behaviors and pretend that their acts are the best for serving the governed political authorities. Let us not forget that the government may seek in some competitions to encourage "Bribe" people to participate in a society experiment and the laws and systems which are not understood by individuals in general. The true reason for corruption may be the desire of the ruling group to have luxury life and paying its expenses which pushed it to deal with corrupted people. The employee may be exposed to pressures from everywhere, by politicians and powerful citizens. Such circumstances may force the employee to subject to these temptations and pressures which makes his behavior contradicts with laws and regulations.

In (Al-Sabagh, 1416 A.H) study entitled with "The effect of political environment on the employee's ethics". It says that the employee, who works in these prevailing political regimes in the Arab world, realizes that the main and actual observation on his behavior at work is his response and subjection to the desires of the executive authority.

Subsequently, the employee sometimes behaviorally seeks to satisfy and meet the desires of the executive authority employees, which represents in the administrative authorities starting from the chief of the organization till the direct chief of the department, in the even if these desires were to the detriment of the employee's personal desires or the public interest.

3- Socioeconomically Reasons:

We may find that many of the values and frameworks of social structure of societies together affect the behavior of the deviated employee such as, allegiance to the clan, sectarianism, position, weakness of allegiance to Home and the absence of social equality and the gap between urban values of a society and the official regulations of work, which approved by the administrative authorities, may lead to the corruption of employee behavior.

Moreover, the material life style brought an era characterized with the deterioration of ethical and social standards. Searching for gaps in regulations and laws (such as, income tax and sales tax) to evade from paying taxes have became a general behavior in many of the Arab states. People start to search for points of weakness in the governmental organizations and nongovernmental ones to achieve personal interests. Consequently, society starts to blink at the immoral acts as long as other individuals did not harmed directly. The one who steals the government is considered as a smart person. Accordingly, we must not expect that the employee's behavior will be immune against these acts in such circumstances.

Furthermore, goods and services which are provided by public authorities in the developing countries are much less than the needs of people. It became familiar to find who pay small amount of money for the governmental employee to get a bed or a seat in a hospital or to use a license...etc. Thus, the lack of public resources leads to the increase of corruption in society. In rich countries, trading in black market is blinked at. The more urgency need for material goods continued, the more goods and services' prices increase. Subsequently, employees face more temptations.

Poor planning for the economic development process according to scientific basis, the absence of feasibility study of the majority of projects, poor distribution of wealth and the decline of per capita income level (PCI) are all reasons lead to the immoral behavior of employee. Thus, bribe, embezzlement, forgery....etc appear.

Economic circumstances, poverty and the decline of wages in some communities make bribe, embezzlement and others acceptable and undeniable acts.

4- Administrative Reasons:

Whenever the administrative authority is characterized with weakness of cultural awareness, there will be cases of administrative corruption represented in the weakness and non integrity of leaderships, poor choice of workers, authorities and responsibilities, non clearness of instructions and poor evaluation of individuals and organizations' performance. Moreover, the absence of written regulations and procedures of work and the records of employees' behavior in the sectors of public and private work pave the way to corruption.

In addition, hyper central and bureaucracy, injustice of distribution of tasks, authorizes and responsibilities, weakness and corrupt of observation authorities, administrative procedures' lag and non coping with the needs of society, weakness and corrupt of employment policies, employing the wrong person in the right position and conflicting laws and systems are all lead to some gaps which encourage corruption and evasion from accountability.

(Dui Vidi, 1981) mentions that if the employees realized that the chance of being punished if they caught during committing illegal act is small, this will make them underestimate of professional ethics and negligence of organizational procedures. Moreover, it will lead to disinterest and negligence between employees, the absence of account system for the behavior and acts of the employee, division of responsibility in somehow to make it difficult to identify the responsible for a certain act and the national command to blink at the immoral activities which are committed by have high positions. All these matters contribute in creating the administrative corruption.

Moreover, historic reasons are one of the reasons administrative and functional deviations. (Abu Shiekha, 1981) indicates that administrative corruption and deviation reasons related to colonization when national employees thought that the embezzlement, waste of money and nepotism are considered as a way of national struggle. They also thought that administrative corruption and deviation are considered as an undermining of the organizations of colonization and damaging them rapidly. They also used (Bribe, Nepotism and abuse of power) as a reason covered by nationality and characterized by tolerance and encouragement by the whole community.

5- Urban Reasons:

Some people think that one of the reasons of the administrative corruption is urban reasons. Urban explanation refers to the gap between urban values of a society and the official regulations of work and approved by the administrative authorities which occur in the developing countries more than the developed ones because of ignorance with characteristic values of urban systems in the societies of developing countries. The change which is brought by the supporters of this point of view cannot shrink the gap between the society and the administrative authority accurately and regularly because the systems of the administrative authorities are quoted from the developed countries in their regular technical and scientific methods to be applied in the reality of the developing countries.

I think that one of the administrative corruption reasons that we quote these systems by their structure and try to apply them without a complete knowledge of their aspects. Subsequently, they are quoted according to their structure not by their right component therefore, corruption appears. This means that administrators set plans and prepare conferences, seminars and meetings as it should be and according to its important. On the other hand, we see that this administrator is the one who does not apply what he says and does because of ignorance, discontentment or something related to his values and personality.

6- Structural Reasons:

Supporters of this structural explanation assert that administrative corruption reasons is a result of the existence of old structures of the state authorities whom do not match with the values and ambitions and also do not meet their requirements and needs. This may lead to a status of noncompliance between the specific administrative authority and those individuals whom make them turn to another ways under the concept of corruption to exceed the limitations of the old structures and achieve self-interests to the detriment of aims and interests of the specific administrative authority.

Impacts of Administrative Corruption:

Corruption in general has a set of negative impacts:

1- Wasting of public funds that can be used in setting up projects that serve citizens because of stealing or wasting it in personal interests.

2- Lack of confidence in the political social regime. Consequently, this leads to the lack of feeling of citizenship and statehood that based on contractual relation between the individual and the state. Moreover, the migration of thinkers and efficiencies that lost hope to get a position fit their abilities that derives them to look for success opportunities outside. Consequently, this affects the economy and the development of the whole society.

3- Poverty, decline of Social Justice, absence of Social and Economical Equality and decline of living standard for many classes in society because of the existence of wealth and authorities under the control of few groups that have money and power to the detriment of the major class which is people.

(El-Shaikhy, 2003) Said: corruption has many destroying and terrifying impacts as follows:

1- Compromising the credibility of the state and lack of confidence in the political regime.

2- Deviation of aims and developmental policies and the direction of general resources to untargeted fields and categories.

3- Wasting some of financial resources through custom and general taxes.

4- Inflating the cost of governmental activities and services.

5- Corruption is one of the reasons of the deficit of the annual balance sheet of the state.

6- Corruption creates distinguish class and conspirator with the society's individuals.

7- Corruption distorts values, justice and principle of equal opportunities.

8- Corruption empties efforts of the governmental administrative reform from its content and effectiveness.

9- Corruption is a factor of escaping of foreign investments.

Moreover, elimination of transparency and breaching justice are also from the impacts of corruption. (Abu Shiekha, 1981) added that among the impacts of unethical behavior that there are some pictures of administrative deviation in Arab countries which most of them:

1- Control of traditional administrative concepts that are concerned only with shape not the content. For example, we find a great concern in the design of the organizational structures regardless the difference between the actual administrative organization and these structures.

2- Stability of administrative organization and its resistance for change and renewal processes.

3- Control of central thought which revealed that higher administrative level makes decisions alone and the absence of authorizing of power that leads to remoteness between the level of making decision and the possibility of applying such decisions by the execution levels.

4- Stereotypy in forming organizations and turning to the method of unifying systems and laws to fit all administrative units regardless the difference of the nature and circumstances of work in each unit.

5- Interference of national authorities that practice planning and observing works in the details of the executive aspects of various affiliated administrative units.

6- Management resorts to hiding its weakness and failure factors through imposing methods of domination steam from monopolization circumstances that it has. It also resorts to aggressive methods in its relation with clients.

7- Occupation of leadership function in the administrative structure in some Arab countries is limited to certain of non-qualified category (Except political loyalty). This category imposed a status of administrative domination and terrorism and paved the way for a climate that helps to opportunism which caused the decline of ethical values and subjective controls established for proper management.

8- Administrative vision is very short whereas it makes urgent decisions when crises occur which later proved to be unscientific.

9- Obvious failure of the management's functions. For planning, it is the first function that is noted to be more concerned by its form against the negligence and ignore of its subject.

10- Management in Arab countries is an example for the traditional bureaucracy which considers routine and models as its aims and not as a mean to achieve targeted desires.

11- We cannot ignore the impact of this behavior that leads to:

A) Huge increasing in the number of authorities without a real reason.

B) Overlapping of specialties and the repetition of performing the same activities between the various governmental authorities.

C) Civil jobs inflation and disguised unemployment.

D) Tending to extravagance in spending money and lack of proper standards in determining expenses.

E) Adhering with the traditional organization methods and old work systems that have been for long years without any amendment.

All of this results from the deviation of management.

Here are some means of administrative anti-corruption as follows:

Administrative Corruption (Unethical Behavior) results when employee tries to be able to abuse his power to achieve some benefits which legally are not for him.

Therefore, we find that it is important to propose and adopt strategy to achieve an effectiveness to abolish administrative corruption.

We can use number of procedures and means to prevent and decrease these unethical behaviors as follows:

• Establishing strict regulations and laws to punish who involved in cases of corruption and strengthening the accountability and transparency systems inside the organizations and society.

• Setting up an independent high committee to investigate in complaints related to corruption issues.

• Follow the policy of general interest and efficiency in appointing any one in administrative positions or any other ones.

• Focusing on prevention measures through reforming the corrupted systems and its prevention for the following:

o Increase the employees' salaries and wages in suitable manner.

o Inspect the periodic acknowledgement of patrimony and the wealth of the employees.

o Transform and exchange employees who are the most vulnerable to unethical behaviors like the employees who are concerned with employment, loans, awarding, license or contracts.

o Be responsible of making decisions related to financial aspects and gain for more than one employee.

o Encourage and create team spirit between governmental employees.

o Include the subject of professional ethics in the educational stages, programs and training courses.

o Formulate and establish the proper regulation such as the Code of Business Conduct to be a guide for the employees.

o Exist of the governmental righteous leader that is considered as an ideal leadership.

• Equalizing before law and accounting the old corrupters before the young ones.

• Offer the policies and programs of the state authorities and the results of its efforts before public.

• Free of Journalism, opinion and speech as an observation tool.

• Establishing a specialized central management for organization and method of work which is based on consulting units in the organizations of the state (Ministries, General Organizations and Local Government Authorities) which mission is as follows:

o Continuances conduct for study of the organizational structures for all public service authorities in the central administration, public organizations and local management to organize to cope with the announced economical and social development plan.

o Conduct important researches and studies to increase production through finding proper climate steam from human respect and assertion of his role.

o Study the followed work methods and ways continuously to simplify it and make it proper for the purposes that it established for to avoid the routine and save time and effort.

We can abstract as follows:

To succeed in applying the strategy, it required to focus and know the basic key which is:

• (Religious Aspect) religious and ethical education is very important because religious aspect has a great effect in self (Behavior of Individual) and the behavior of the group (Members). The previous procedures cannot be achieved unless with complying with professional ethics steam from the wise religious values.

• The possibility of applying such previous procedures that agrees with the nature of Islamic instructions. It cannot be achieved unless we complied with applying it that means the necessity of complying with the Islamic religious law till we execute it. Accordingly, commitment with these procedures requires adherence to the Islamic religious law which never come to wrong and came to fix humanity.

• The necessity of establishing the professional ethics to improve the employee's behavior and his performance and organization's performance and develops his community.

(Chapter Four)

Ethics of Function & Employee in Islam

1- Ethics and Faith

2- Work in Islam

3- Functional Ethics in Islam

4- Employee's Ethics in Islam

<u>**Ethics and Belief**</u>:

Belief is the resource of ethic's value. First order that is required from the adult person is to "To testify that there is no god but Allah". If he believed in it and what this testimony requires of other pillars, he will be asked to practice the other provisions of Islamic religious law and to have good ethics.

Belief is the basic for the acceptance of work by Allah and creed is the pillar which moral, social and other Islamic systems were based on.

Belief is related to human behavior and relationship with others which means that belief is related to ethics that shows in the behavior of Muslim.

There are many texts from Quran and Sunnah point out the relation between belief and ethics as follows:

- Allah the Highest says: **{O you who have believed, fear Allah and be with those who are true}** (AT-TAWBAH- 119).

- Abu Huraira (May Allah be pleased with him) reported: Prophet-PBUH- said: **{Whoever believes in Allah and the Last Day should talk what is good or keep quiet, and whoever believes in Allah and the Last Day should not hurt (or insult) his neighbor; and whoever believes in Allah and the Last Day, should entertain his guest generously}.**

- Anas reported that the Prophet-PBUH- said: **{None amongst you believes (truly) until he loves for his brother"- or he said "For his neighbour"- "That which he loves for himself.}.** (Sahih Muslim, Book of Faith, Hadith No. (45), part No. (1).

- Anas reported that the Prophet-PBUH- said: **{Belief of any person does not straight till his heart does}.** (Narrated by Imam Ahmed in Musnadu (198\3),(13071), and al-Khara'iti in ethics generosities(442).

- Prophet -PBUH- said: **{Nothing is heavier on the believer's Scale on the Day of Judgment than good character. For indeed Allah, The Most High, is angered by the shameless obscene person}.** (Sahih at-Tirmidhi, part No. (8), Book of Righteousness and Maintaining Good Relations with Relatives).

<u>**We note from the previous texts as follows:**</u>

1- These previous texts are for believers and that having righteousness of ethics is believer's characteristics.

2- Ethics is like a body and belief is the heart because monotheism is belief's base and its fruit is to free man from self-standard regardless of their power and purify heart from desires, tendencies and fills it with the light of right and belief.

3- Belief is the work of heart that controls all feelings. The sign of belief appears on man's behavior and improve his treatment with others. This behavior is resulting from ethics.

4- If the heart is straight, belief will also straight and then Muslim's behavior will be defined in all his worships and dealing and this behavior is improved. This will appear through ethics which is the Behavior determinants.

5- Ethics is the base for the righteousness of all works of the individual which indicates the importance of good ethics for man.

6- Belief determines ethical behavior for it is a motivated power for the good morals of man according to Allah's instructions. Then, there will be an internal balance in the human soul between self and belief.

- Prophet-PBUH- said: {If your sin makes you sad and your charity makes you happy, then you are a believer}. (Musnad Imam Ahmed No. (22552), p.641).

(Draz, 1973, p.249) said that the inside blame's degree to ourselves reflects our belief and measures it accurately. We feel how big and dangerous our sin is spottily and according to our feeling's degree with responsibility.(p.249).

7- Having ethics steams from heart as Prophet-PBUH- said: {Truly in the body there is a morsel of flesh, which, if it be whole, all the body is whole, and which, if it is diseased, all of [The body] is diseased. Truly, it is the heart.} (Narrated by Bukhari & Muslim, Sahih Al-Bukhari & Muslim, al-lu'lu'wal-marjan, part No. (4). If belief settled in the heart, it will be reflected through conducting what pleases Allah.

Prophet-PBUH- said: {Modesty and belief are together. If one of them is removed, the other is removed} (Narrated by Al- Hakim in Al-Mustadrak, No. (66), p.20).

8- Purification of the heart insures the health of the whole body, i.e., the purification of the Muslim employee's heart insures his body's health (With his deeds).

- Prophet-PBUH-said: {Heart is like a king and has soldiers. If the king is good, his soldiers become good and if he gets spoilt, his soldiers get spoilt} (Narrated by Al-Bayhaqi, Al-Suyuti mentioned in Al-jamea2\89).

(Draz, 1973) mentioned a wise comment: "If the heart spoiled, don't let his prayers, feast or any extremities deceive you because if all of his extremities have obeyed Allah and his extremities decided to do good deeds, then the extremities still breaking and the heart is vain, so what is showed on these extremities?. If the heart is rich and extremities are broken, the less movement of the heart can spread a great righteousness.

We can find that, if the heart of the Muslim employee is good, his work and performance will be subjected to the orders of Allah in a high quality and mastering.

9- Belief is the work of the heart. There must be a sign for this belief in the behavior of Muslim employee. Accordingly, we find him deals in a good manner with others. Believer observes Allah in each word and deed. During conducting his work there will be will (Firm) and intention. If he intended Allah's please when working, it will be truly for Allah.

10- The matter here concerns with comparing between the heart and body's movement. (Draz, 1973) mentioned that Islamic ethics is like the heart of the body.

– Allah the Highest says: **{Those [among them] who believed in Allah and the Last Day and did righteousness- will have their reward with their Lord, and no fear will there be concerning them, nor will they grieve.}**. (AL-BAQARAH, 62)

– Allah the Highest says: **{Indeed, those who have believed and those who have emigrated and fought in the cause of Allah- those expect the mercy of Allah. And Allah is Forgiving and Merciful}**. (AL-BAQARAH,218)

– Allah the Highest says: **{And do not approach immoralities- what is apparent of them and what is concealed. And do not kill the soul which Allah has forbidden [to be killed] except by [legal] right. This has He instructed you that you may use reason.}**.(AL-AN'AM,151)

– Allah the Highest says: **{But whoever desires the Hereafter and exerts the effort due to it while he is a believer- it is those whose effort is ever appreciated [by Allah]}** (AL-ISRA, 19)

Accordingly Quran doesn't praise the work that does not steam from deep of the soul. It shows mostly the success of heart work only whether by considering its value as Allah the Highest says: **{Indeed, those who lower their voices before the Messenger of Allah- they are the ones whose hearts Allah has tested for righteousness. For them is forgiveness and great reward}** (Al-Hujurat, 3).

- Allah the Highest says: **{That [is so]. And whoever honors the symbols of Allah- indeed, it is from the piety of hearts}** (Al-Hajj. 32).

By considering it as essential term to for belief as Allah the Highest says: **{Who feared the Most Merciful unseen and came with a heart returning [in repentance]}** (Qaf, 33).

- Allah the Highest says: **{But only one who comes to Allah with a sound heart}** (Ash-Shu'ar, 89)

Belief is a term to work validity and acceptance. This work appears through the employee's behavior that relates to these behaviors and his treatment with others which is called employee's ethics.

<u>**We can extract that as follows:**</u>

• Islamic system generally is established on its ethical principles. Ethics is the essence of the heavenly religions. Prophet-PBUH-said: **{I was sent to perfect honorable morals}.** (Al-Muwatta (3357), Narrated by Ahmed(2\381).

Therefore, the purpose of his message is to complete and adjustment ethics and the purpose for all messages is ethical because the religion itself is good morals.

• For ethics is important, we find it equal to creed whereas Allah and his Messenger connect between belief and good morals in Hadith **when the Messenger was asked, {who is the best believer?} He answered {who has good ethics}** (Authenticate by Abu Dawud and At-Tirmidhi and Al-Nasā'ī in Book of Al-Mugni,1\931)

• Islam considered belief as righteousness, Allah the Highest says: **{Righteousness is not that you turn your faces toward the east or the west, but [true] righteousness is [in] one who believes in Allah , the Last Day, the angels, the Book, and the prophets and gives wealth, in spite of love for it, to relatives, orphans, the needy, the traveler, those who ask [for help], and for freeing slaves; [and who] establishes prayer and gives zakah; [those who] fulfill their promise when they promise; and [those who] are patient in poverty and hardship and during battle. Those are the ones who have been true, and it is those who are the righteous}** (Al-BAQARAH, 177) and the Prophet-PBUH-said: **{Virtue is noble behavior}.**(Narrated by Muslim, Book of Righteousness and Maintaining Good Relations with Relatives,2553).

Virtue is a characteristic of ethical deed. It is a comprehensive name for all kinds of goodness.

• Therefore, there is a great bond between ethics and belief as we find it between ethics and worshiping whereas worshiping is a spiritual ethics in essence to perform divine duties. We find it in dealings which are the second part of the Islamic religious law clearly.

We can see that the aspects of Islam connected with an ethical bond to achieve an ethical aim that assure that ethics is the essence of Islam and the Islamic legislation system is the body of this ethical spirit.

<u>**Work in Islam:**</u>

Work means movement or effort that man does by his mind in case of understanding or by his body as his legs or hands. This means that work has two pillars:

1- Outside movement that man does by his organs or mind.

2- Inside motivation that directs such movement which is intention or belief (Mimeni, 1414 A.H, P.31).

- Allah the Highest says: {**And who is better in speech than one who invites to Allah and does righteousness and says, "Indeed, I am of the Muslims**} (FUSSILAT, 33)

Allah ordered us with work where he says: {**Do [as you will], for Allah will see your deeds, and [so, will] His Messenger and the believers. And you will be returned to the Knower of the unseen and the witnessed, and He will inform you of what you used to do**} (AT-TAWBAH, 105)

 Allah speaks to his Messenger about this matter saying: {**So when you have finished [your duties], then stand up [for worship]**} (Ash-Shura, 7).

Prophet-PBUH-said: {**Work for your life as if you will live forever, and work for your hereafter as if you will die tomorrow**}.

Prophet-PBUH-praises worker saying: {**He who comes the evening is tired of the work of his hands is he who receives absolution**} (Narrated by Al-Tabarani (worker's treasure 4\7) Almasder Alrabih (306).

Prophet-PBUH- said: {**Nobody has ever eaten a better meal than that which one has earned by working with one's own hands. The Prophet of Allah, David used to eat from the earnings of his manual labor**} (Narrated by Al-Bukhari, Book ok Sales and Trade No. (14), part No. (3).

In another narration: {**No man earns anything better than that which he earns with his own hands**} (Narrated by Ibn Majah, Sahih Al-jamea (5660).

Ancestors realized the importance of work in life to prepare for hereafter, and Ali (May Allah be pleased with him) said: {**we work today without judgment and tomorrow we will be judged without work**} (Sahih Al-Bukhari, Book of Slaves No (4), part No. (8).

Islam is the religion of work. It promotes with work to religious duties whereas belief is connected with good deed that is useful for the individual and groups together. There is no verse in Quran that mentions belief without work.

<u>**Characteristics of work in Islam:**</u>

Islam is religion of work that makes work as a duty upon Muslims and accordingly, Islam establishes some characteristics and controls to work that achieve this as follows:

1- Belief & Good Work (Deed):

Islam is a creed and work and this is what Quran assures in more than 50 verses that connect belief with good work (deed) whether in individual or group form. (Abdelhady, 1975) said that belief is certainties and believable in a certain idea or behavior. Doing good deeds mean the absolute good work that benefits all individuals and groups whether in the affairs of life or religion. Quran connects between belief and good work like the connection between origin and branch and the base with the structure which one of them cannot be without the other. Islam does not know belief that does not concern with good work and does not steam from a doctrine.

2- Work and intention:

As we all know, the intention is an important thing in deeds. Any Muslim employee has to be sincere in his intention for seeking the pleasure of Allah while he doing his work. (Mimeni, 1994) says that; the Muslim has to ask himself this question, why would I do this work? If his intention was for someone rather than Allah, he should change his intention and clear it for Allah. When the Muslim employee does any work, his intention of this work must be sincere for the pleasure of Allah only. The Muslim has to learn the good intention at any work he does. Muslim has to his deed and knowledge for help his religion and protects it in a good way. The Muslim has to make his conscience as an observer upon him at all deeds and words he says by remembering that Allah observers you at all times. So that will help him to become faithfully in any deed or works he does because of Allah notes and sees all sins of his creatures and know everything about them. The responsible may miss or forget anything but Allah does not forget or miss anything, as (Abdelhady, 1975) says: the intention is too important to define the deeds and judge them: Allah the Highest says: **{each works according to his manner, but your Lord is most knowing of who is best guided in way.} (Al-'Isra' 84).**

In this purpose, al-imam Al-Bukhari (Sahih Al-Bukhari) sad that the meaning of "on his own" in the previous verse means "his intention". Allah the Highest says: {**And for everyone is a direction for which he turns. So race in goodness. And wherever you are, Allah will bring you all together. He has power over all things} (Al-Baqarah, 148).**

As the prophet Mohamed -BPUH- says: {the reward of deeds depends upon the intentions and every person will get the reward according to what he has intended. So whoever emigrated for worldly benefits or for a woman to marry, his emigration was for what he emigrated for.} (In Sahih Al-Bukhari, Revelation, (1) chapter, part 1).

The previous Hadith by the prophet Mohamed –BPUH- which wrote and kept by Al-Bukhari in his book of the Hadith-Sharif (Sahih Al-Bukhari) which refers to the deed and work does not mean anything without the intention, Which also means the deeds are not become (morally) without the intention.

As what (Draz, 1973) said: we cannot decide that our inward thoughts have not any effect at our emergent deeds. From this point, the intention is the basis of any work and behaviors, as well as, it is considered the basic of morals. As Allah, the Highest says: {**Say: 'I am only a human like you, revealed to me is that your God is One God. Let him who hopes for the encounter with his Lord do good work, and not associate anyone with the worship of his Lord.} '(Al-Kahf, 110).**

In this purpose Ibn Qayyim says that: The heart deeds are the intended asset and the organs deeds are complementary, the intention as the soul or comes from the soul, acts of the deeds as the body organs thus if the body spreads or leaves the soul will die, and the deeds without intention will be considered nothing. We deduce that knowing the heart roles are more important than organs roles and the heart is the original but the organs based on the heart.

3- The perfect work and deed:

Islam order us to do the work in a good manner, as which referred in some verses such as Allah the Highest says: {It is He who created the heavens and the earth in six days and His Throne was upon the waters that He might try you, (and see) which of you excel in works.} This verse means that Allah who created the human, life, and death just for testing the human being by their deeds and how they make their deed in a good manner in their life (Hud, 7).

Allah says: {**We have appointed all that is on the earth an adornment for it, in order that we try which of them is finest in works.}** (Al-Kahf, 7); and says: {**who created death and life that He might examine which of you is best in deeds, and He is the Almighty, the Forgiving}** (Al-Mulk.2)

Doing the work in its perfect manner means the worker is required to do his working in the perfect manner. Although our religious solicits us to improve our performance at the work or any deed, not only improve it but to do this work in its perfect manner, as Allah the Highest says: {**And you see the mountains, you think them to be solid, and they shall pass away as** the passing away of the cloud- the handiwork of Allah who has made everything thoroughly; surely He is Aware of what you do} (An- Naml, 88); also Allah says {**Had Allah willed, He would have made you one nation. But He leads astray whomsoever He will and gives guidance to whomsoever He will. You shall be questioned about what you did**} (An-Nahl, 93).

Allah ordered to reward the workers for doing their work in its perfect manner as Allah said:{ **As for those who believe and do good works We do not waste the wage of whosoever does good works**} (Al-Kahf, 30); also Allah says: {**that Allah will recompense them for the finest deeds they did and increase them from His bounty. Allah provides without measure to whom He will**} (An-Nur).

the prophet Mohamed -PBUH- instructs and solicits us to work in a good way and to do our works in its perfect manner, as the prophet-PBUH- said {**Allah will be pleased with those who try to do their work in a perfect way**} (Narrated by Al- bihiki in fied Al- kadier book, No.1861, p.2). Prophet-PBUH- said about improving the work that: {**Allah will be pleased with those who try to improve their works**} (Al- bihiki narrated, in fied Al- kadier book, No.1861, p.2), also he said {**May Allah have mercy for those who do their works perfectly**} (Saeed Al- Khudri, Jami Al- Oswol, 11\158, P. 8716)

There are some things does not exist in the perfect work such as, fraud, liar, unfaithfulness or non-complying with the promise because these things are Incompatible with the work sincerity which is considered one of the important terms in the perfect work; as Allah said {**Believers, do not betray Allah and the Messenger, nor knowingly betray your trust**} (Al-Anfal, 27)

(Abdelhady, 1973) says that for the (Staif functions) which depends on saying the advice and the technical opinion; it needs to ask the expertise, specialist, and scientist as what Allah the highest says: {**If you supplicate to them they cannot hear your supplication, and if they heard, they cannot answer you. On the Day of Resurrection, they will disown your associating. None can tell you like He who is the Aware'** (Fatir, 14); and Allah also says: {**We never sent but men before you to whom We revealed, ask the people of the Remembrance, if you do not know**} (An-Nahl, 43)); and Allah also says; {**When a matter comes to them, be it of security or fear, they broadcast it, whereas if they returned it to the Messenger and to those in authority among them, those of them whose task is to research it would have** known it. If it was not for the Bounty of Allah and His Mercy, all but a few of you would have followed satan} (An-Nisa, 83).

From this verses above, Islam order us to ask the specialist and expertise at the unknowable matter to us or anything we do not know.

So the Islam solicits us to excel the work by calling for improving the deeds and works perform or to ask the expertise, specialist, and scientist for advising.

4- Facilitating and simplifying the deed or work as we can (facilitating the work or deed as we can).

One of the Islamic features that ensuring the physical capacity idea for working as an obligate term. Islam does not ask or order us to make a difficult thing or act; as Allah the Highest says: **{Let the rich spend according to his wealth and for he whose provision is little, let him spend from what Allah has given him. Allah does not charge a soul except with that He has given him. Surely, Allah will bring ease after difficulty}** (At-Talaq, 7); Allah the Highest says: **{Allah charges no soul except to its capacity. For it is what it has earned, and against it what it has gained. 'Our Lord, do not take us to account if we have forgotten, or made a mistake. Our Lord, do not burden us with a load as you have burdened those before us. Our Lord, do not overburden us with more than we can bear. And pardon us, and forgive us, and have mercy on us. You are our Guide, so give us victory over the nation, the unbelievers}** (Al-Baqarah, 286)

Islam is caring about the abilities of the human (employee) and his capability in the assignment. According to the previous verses, we can see that Allah makes the assignment according to our capacity. So the worker must not make a work or deed which leads to his end or that can harm him or that one that makes him suffering from damage or loss.

(Draz, 1973) says that the assignment comes to the human according to his ability and capacity. So we can see that; the Islamic values neglect any of difficult or hard assignment which is considered as more than human capability; as it also neglects any discomfort may exhaust the human power or their power limitation.

As Allah says: {the month of Ramadan is the month in which the Koran was sent down, a guidance for people, and clear verses of guidance and the criterion. Therefore, whoever of you witnesses the month, let him fast. But he who is ill, or on a journey shall (fast) a similar number (of days) later on. Allah wants ease for you and does not want hardship for you. And that you fulfill the number of days and exalt Allah who has guided you in order that you be thankful} (Al-Baqarah, 185); Allah also says: **{Struggle for Allah as is due to Him. He has chosen you and has not laden a burden upon you in your religion, being the Creed of Abraham your father. He has named you Muslims before and in this so that the Messenger (Muhammad) can be a witness for you, and in order that you be witnesses against mankind. Therefore, establish the prayer and pay the obligatory charity and hold fast to Allah. He is your Guardian, the Excellent Guardian, the Excellent Helper}** (Al-Hajj, 78); Allah also says: **{Allah wishes to lighten for you (the jurisprudence), and humans are created weak'** (An-Nisa, 28) and **'We have not sent you (Prophet Muhammad) except as a mercy to all the worlds}** (AL-ANBYA, 107).

In the previous verses; we see another grace that Allah sad before about the ability in the work and deeds; one of the working features in the Islam is to work according to your capacity. As you can find in the previous verses another feature of the work which is the simple. According to the history, we find that the ease is relevant to the Islamic nation.

Although the assignment idea (capacity) is a feature may exist and relevant to all fair and acceptable Ethical doctrines which come in the Islamic religion, but it means the ease at the work. As (Draz, 1973) says in his book "The ethics constitute in the holy Quran" this side is not common between all doctrines and we can see that from what Allah says: **{Allah charges no soul except to its capacity. For it is what it has earned, and against it what it has gained. 'Our Lord, do not take us to account if we have forgotten, or made a mistake. Our Lord, do not burden us with a load as you have burdened those before us. Our Lord, do not overburden us with more than we can bear. And pardon us, and forgive us, and have mercy on us. You are our Guide, so give us victory over the nation, the unbelievers}** (AL-BAQARAH, 286). By this verse, we can deduce that; there was a difficult way in other ideology. So we can say that Mohamed religious or the Islam is considered perfect religion and very good religion because it consists of the ease rather than the difficulty.

Some of the ease aspects in the work which ordered by the Quran such as refraining from hyperbole in making worshipful deeds or works as advised us not to commit this hyperbole, excessive or exaggeration.

(Draz, 1973) says in his book "The ethics constitute in the Quran" (It is known that in the beginning of the prophet message was ordered to spend a large portion of the night in the pray and recite the Quran as Allah says: **{Rise (to pray) the night except a little, half the night,** or a little less, r a little more; and with recitation, recite the Koran.} (AL-MUZZAMMIL, 2-4).

in addition, the Companions of the Prophet followed his guidance as they used to do what he does. When we read the end of the verse we will find a directed lesson which attracts the attention to that if they could not practice this rite in previous verse because of raising or existing a certain circumstances, such as illness, travel, and Jihad (Fight for the way of Allah) then the prophet tells them to do the voluntary prayer at night as they can, as Allah says: **{Say: 'I supplicate only to my Lord and I do not associate any with Him}** (Al-Jinn, 20).

This religion gives the full exemption for those who can't work, it also exempts the incapable or incompetents and people of the Jihad duty, as Allah says: **{There is no fault in the blind, or the lame, or the sick. He who obeys Allah and His Messenger He shall admit him to Gardens underneath which rivers flow; but he who turns away shall be punished with a painful punishment}** (ALFATH, 17).

The Islam permitted to the vulnerable people on the earth who should have to look for a safe shelter to practice their freedom of belief and worship, as permitted to them to stay as where they are as long as they have no means of migration; in that purpose Allah says: **{Except the men, women, and children who, being abased have no means and they are unable to guide themselves to a way}** (AN-NISA, 98). As Allah speaks about shortening the pray during the travel, as in the verse **{when you are journeying in the land, there is no fault in you that you shorten the prayer if you fear that those who disbelieve will afflict you. Indeed, the unbelievers are a clear enemy for you}** (AN-NISA, 101).

As the Quran speaks about that; the people are obligated to fast in a specific time but for the travelers and patients they can fast in the days ahead (when they be able to fast), as Allah the Highest says: **{The month of Ramadan is the month in which the Koran was sent down, a guidance for people, and clear verses of guidance and the criterion. Therefore, whoever of you witnesses the month, let him fast. But he who is ill, or on a journey shall (fast) a similar number (of days) later on. Allah wants ease for you and does not want hardship for you. And that you fulfill the number of days and exalt Allah who has guided you in order that you be thankful}** (Al-BAQARAH, 185)

if the traveler does not find a water to purify and clean himself or the patient who suffers from a daises that he can't use water with it should use a clean earthen or sand to wipe or rub his face and hands with it (which considered more an easier way) as Allah says: **{But if you are sick or traveling, or, if when you have just relieved yourselves or had intercourse**

with women and you cannot find water, touch the clean surface of the earth and rub your hands and faces with it} (AL MA'IDA, 6).

It is worth mentioning that; these examples are referring to the practical ease which emphasizes or asserts the mercy of this religion and it's privileging. If this mercy and ease in the worship; so what about the work? By the way, Allah facilitates the works and assignments according to our capacity which refers to there is a simplicity in our works not only the worship. From this point, we deduce that; Allah tells ordered us to be merciful and treating people in a good manner.

These works feature in Islam so the mercy of this religion including the work accordingly to the general human nature and facilitate to be suitable for our life which is not considered as an authoritarian work.

The study of (Abdul Latif, 2006) emphasizes that; multitude, complexity, and lack of simplifying the procedures and its length steps are one of the administrative corruption causes. Islam comes to facilitate and keep the matters or things too easier for people.

5- Determines and arranges the duties:

One of the Islamic advantages is making the compulsory works and duties too easy and possible to do. When we see the employees we find that; all people have neither the same the militancy nor energy morality. From this point we deduce that; the soul that has a good will and strong determination will keep their duties in the possible highest perfection point.

The human (Workers) like any system of relationships which divided into the vital element, personal, family, and humanitarian is related elements can be progressed and improved. So how we can make all of these aspects at a particular level?

The concept of Islamic is what the prophet sad-PBUH- says: **{You owe a duty to your (God), you owe a duty to your body; you owe a duty to your family; so you should give to everyone his due}** (Sahih Al- Bukhari, 1968).

So, can we hint the upper limit which is different from each one other? How we define the necessary minimum in our duties or deeds with Allah or ourselves?

In Islam, we find a specific and a distinctive into the pillars, assignments, duties, and making the limitations. Also, Allah puts the main assignment and duty firstly then the other assignments and the deeds or works which increase its reward. Then Allah arranges the (Forbidden) sins, then the other evil deeds then immoralities or abominations. Also, Allah distinguishes between two types of the permissible deeds and works which mean the permitted deeds or works and the condoned or tolerated deeds or works. We deduce that; there are gradual values, and the Islamic mind has to be aware and be able to understand this diversity and how to use permitted and tolerated deeds or works.

From here comes the meaning of determining the obligated works and duties besides arranging them according to its significance. One of the important things is to define the work type and its responsibilities or duties, its significance, and the permitted period to achieve this work. Therefore, the man will be asked about the works and deed for which he made after defining and grading the work or deed. Here comes the knowledge theory; so that the worker has to know what he has to do, and how to do the works and duties priorities in a perfect manner.

You should determine the working wage with its time, amount, and his role in the work to take it. Furthermore; the work has to be clear and transparency that will help the responsible to achieve the justice which is considered as the work feature in Islam.

Informing and defining the responsibilities which related to the employee lead to avoid the mistakes at the work performance. in the other hand; But lacking obligations and responsibilities 'clarity leads to exempt the employee from the penalty which leads to the corruption in the work and not achieve the perfection in his work performance.

So the clarity of duties and its arrangements give the worker Muslim the work ethics and moralities which are ordered by our Islam. So he performs his duties in a faithfully and in a good manner to achieve the work's perfection.

We can deduce that:

* Islam is consists of believe and work.

- The work Pillars in Islam:

* The external movement which made by the human organs (Worker)

* The oriented internal motivation to this movement which means the intention

-The work features in Islam

* The faith and good work or deed

* The work (deed) and intention

* The excellent work

* Facilitating the work according to the capacity

* Determining the works and their arrangement

We find that the work features in Islam depending on the work pillars in Islam which are the external movement (Virtual movement), internal motivation (inside the human):

*** Faith and good work**: Is the internal motivation (Virtual movement) by human organs.

*** Work and intention**: The intention is the internal motivation for the virtual work by the work organs. The excellent work can't be achieved by the external movement to the man organs only, but the work needs to the positive power by the faith and internal intention.

*** Facilitating work and deed as possible which means that any of the assignments will suitable the human abilities**: The worker ordered to work according to the capacity of his organs external movement. Also, the worker is working to facilitate his assignments to achieve the required work in a good way by using the organs external movement only, but by using internal motivation from the positive intention and faith.

*** Finally determining the works and their arrangement:**

It is made by using the worker man organs (Virtual movement) so the Islam solicits on the importance of determining the works and the appeared duties by the worker to make them in the best way and achieving the required work in a good way. That needs to the internal power (Internal) power of the faith and good intention at work so the excelled work will be achieved in a good way.

Then these features are considered as an ethics base in the Islamic working. From this point; these features are an ethics base comes from several morals inside the Moslem employee and if he obligated to these morals; he will achieve the required work in its perfect manner.

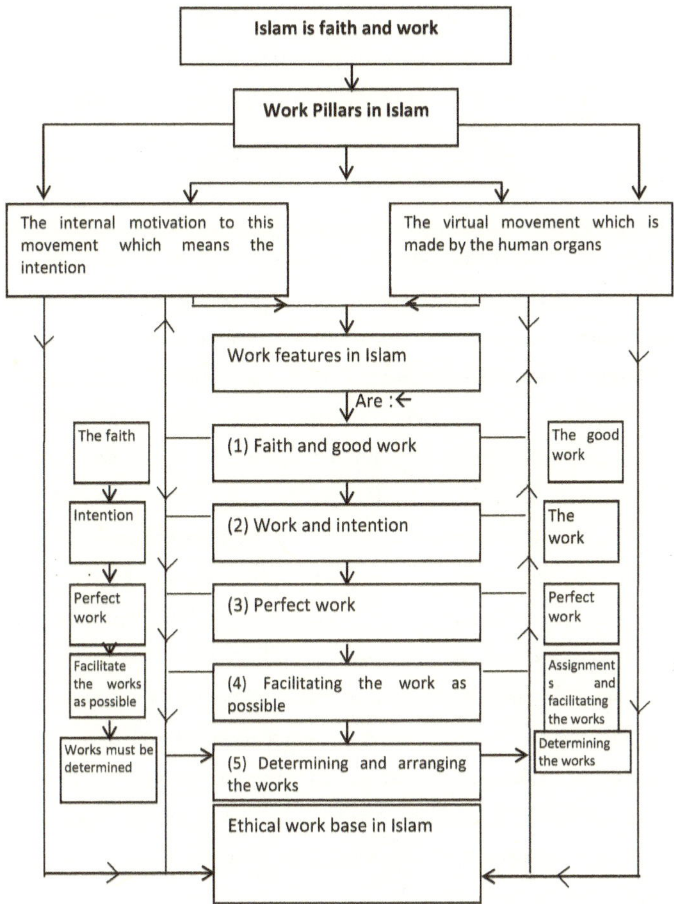
Islam is faith and work
Work Pillars in Islam
The internal motivation to this movement which means the intention
The virtual movement which is made by the human organs
Work features in Islam
Are :
The faith
The good work
(1) Faith and good work
Intention
The work
(2) Work and intention
Perfect work
Perfect work
(3) Perfect work
Facilitate the works as possible
Assignments and facilitating the works
(4) Facilitating the work as possible
Works must be determined
Determining the works
(5) Determining and arranging the works
Ethical work base in Islam

<u>**Functional Ethics in Islam**</u>

Functional Ethics in Islam are not a new creation but they are original Islamic values which come from "holy Quran" and Sunnah (What Prophet Mohamed 'peace upon him' said) with what solicited by our religious of a good ethics principles and basics. The work in Islam is related to the ethics and Islamic morals which lead to achieving the work performance in its best manner.

Functional Ethics: the most importance ethics are as the follows:

<u>**1- The function is a trust:**</u>

Allah the Highest says: **{Allah orders you all to hand back trusts to their owners, and when you judge between people you judge with justice. Indeed, the best is the exhortation with which Allah exhorts you. Allah is the Hearer, the Seer, Believers, obey Allah and obey the Messenger and those in authority among you. Should you dispute about anything refer it to Allah and the Messenger, if you believe in Allah and the Last Day. That is better and the best interpretation}** (AN-NISA', 58, 59); and says **{Those who believe and migrated, and fought for the Cause of Allah with their wealth and their persons; and those who sheltered them and helped them shall be guided to each other. And those who believe, but have not emigrated you have any guidance towards them till they emigrate. But if they seek your help in the cause of your religion, it is your duty to help them, except against a nation with whom you have a treaty. Allah sees the things you do.}** (AL-'ANFAL, 72)

This concept appears when the honored companion Abu Dharr al-Ghifari asked the prophet that: **{I said to Messenger of Allah: "Why do you not appoint me to an (official) position?" He-PBUH- patted me on the shoulder with his hand and said, "O Abu Dharr, you are a weak man and it is a trust and it will be a cause of disgrace and remorse on the Day of Resurrection except for the one who takes it up with a full sense of responsibility and fulfills what is entrusted to him (discharges its obligations efficiently}** (Narrated by Muslim, No. 1825). In addition, Abu Huraira narrated that **{The prophet said, when honesty is lost, then wait for the Hour." It was asked, "How will honesty be lost, O Allah's Messenger?" He said, "When authority is given to those who do not deserve it, then wait for the Hour.}** (Al- Bukhari Narrated, No. 59).

That refers to the Muslim who has a function will be responsible for his work and will be asked about it in the afterlife, as Allah says **{Say: 'Allah will see your works and so will His**

Messenger and the believers; then you shall be returned to the Knower of the unseen and the visible, and He will inform you of what you were doing} (AT-TAUBAH, 105).

Islam is considering that doing the work in its perfect manner with honesty is one of employee responsibilities whatever his administrative level. So the employee has to choose the function which is suitable for himself and his abilities to do it in its perfect manner. The director or any who has the authorities has to honest when choosing the employee for the work. In this purpose; (Ibn Taymiyyah, D.T, P.7) said that "The responsible manager or chief in the work must choose the Muslim who has the most abilities to do this work in its perfect manner" and he quoted that from what the prophet -PBUH- said: **{Who appoints any one of Muslims to take something or rule he wants shall be considered a betrayer to Allah, his Messenger, and the believers}**. (Al- Hakm Narrated in his Sahih, Al- Mostdrk, 4\ 92- 93, No. 1462).

As Omar Ibn Al- Khattab said **{Who assigns the Muslims for a relationship or friendly ship will be considered a betrayer to Allah, his Messenger, and the believers}** (Ibn Taymiyyah, D. T, 8).

Ibn Taymiyyah also cleared in his book (Legitimate political) that (We must choose the man who can make the work at the best way not choosing him according to his request of working or being him the first of requisition) and he quoted by what the prophet-PBUH-, when two of people asked him to rule a state or work in something that Allah granted you then the prophet said: **{We do not assign the authority of ruling to those who ask for it, nor to those who are keen to have it.}**.

Muslim should not appoint anyone for the purposes of a relationship or a friendship.

<u>2- The function is an assignment and duties not honorably or easy to anyone so it must be given for who has the capacity to perform it in its perfect manner:</u>

As Abu Musa al-Ashari said for this purpose: **{Two men from my tribe and I entered upon the Prophet. One of the two men said to the Prophet, "O Allah's Messenger-PBUH-! Appoint me as a governor," and so did the second. The Prophet -PBUH- said, "We do not assign the authority of ruling to those who ask for it, nor to those who are keen to have it}** (Sahih Muslim 1733, Bab Al- Amarah, Al- Bukhari Narrated, Bab Al- Ahkam).

People must know that their functions do not belong to anyone because this function or work consists of assignments which must be done. So this function is not an honorable thing. as we saw In the previous Hadith by Abu Dharr Al- Ghfare who asked the prophet to assign him to rule a state but the prophet did not assign him because of lacking the enough capability to rule it. The person must be qualified to be appointed in any function. Persons have to be appointed upon the abilities, merits, honesty, and justice.

The personal must be appointed in the function according to his ability to make its duties. Furthermore, he must execute people's interests and not, disrupting their interests. Function is a service used to satisfy the needs of the physical and psychological citizens; as the Prophet-PBUH- said {**If Allah invests to someone the affairs of the Muslims and he (i.e., the ruler) ignores their rights, denies their access to him and neglects their needs, Allah will not answer his prayer or realize his hopes and will act towards him with indifference on the Day of Resurrection**} (Abi Dawud Narrated, Sahih Targhib, 2208).

(Abu Sin, 1996) says that the public office consists of assignments must be and to keep working at this office or function depends on expiration of the incumbent period. So we deduce that this office is not a property to the worker. Then who sees that function is not suitable to him; in this case, he must leave it whatever his position. May the person who cannot direct his work at the best way because of lacking in the intellectual or body ability to do the function or maybe because of betraying and his function's performance is being without honesty.

The prophet-PBUH- and Omar Bin Khattab isolated a number of workers and employees for mere suspicion of their unfaithfulness or lacking of efficiency, competence to performance the public office or function. The Prophet isolated Ala bin Hadrami at his ruling to Bahrain because by Wafd Abdul Qais complained to the Prophet then He appointed Aban Ibn Saeed rather than him and the Prophet told Aban that (Help them in a good way and solve their problems).

Allah's Messenger-PBUH- employed an employee (To collect Zakat). The employee returned after completing his job and said, **{O Allah's Messenger-PBUH-! This (amount of Zakat) is for you, and this (Another amount) was given to me as a present." The Prophet-PBUH- said to him, "Why didn't you stay at your father's or mother's house and see if you would be given presents or not?" Then Allah's Messenger-PBUH- got up in the evening after the prayer, and having testified that none has the right to be worshiped but Allah and praised and glorified Allah as He deserved, he said, "Now then! What about an employee whom we employ and then he comes and says, 'This amount (of Zakat) is for you, and this (Amount) was given to me as a present'? Why didn't he stay at the house of his father and mother to see if he would be given presents or not? By Him in Whose Hand Muhammad's soul is, none of you** will steal anything of it (i.e. Zakat) but will bring it by carrying it over his neck on the Day of Resurrection. If it has been a camel, he will bring it (Over his neck) while it will be grunting, and if it has been a cow, he will bring it (Over his neck), while it will be mooing; and if it has been a sheep, he will bring it (Over his neck) while it will be bleeding." The Prophet-PBUH- added, "I have preached you (Allah's Message)." Abu Humaid said, "the Allah's Messenger-PBUH- raised his hands so high that we saw the whiteness of his armpits.}

Islam instructs us that do not assign the work to those who are not have the capacity and efficiency for this work, as Allah says in the words of Joseph {**He (Joseph) said: 'Give me charge of the storehouses of the land, I am a knowledgeable guardian}** (The Prophet Joseph -Yusuf, 55). When we see when the Prophet Joseph said {**I am a knowledgeable guardian**} we will find these words referring to the competence to be responsible for the land storehouses of Egypt.

The prophet-PBUH- and his companions took into account this matter with regard to the mandates and responsibilities. So they put every worker in the right and suitable, for example, as indicated in the (AL- kows, D.T) that the Prophet-PBUH- chose Moaz Ibn Gabal to assign him to judge between Yemen's people according to his juries and wisdom as chose Massaba Ibn Amir to help the people and advice them in Islam for his wisdom, knowledge, and his good manner. The Prophet-PBUH- chose Omar Ibn Al-Khattab as an employee to collect the charity (Zakat) for his justice and strength of personality. Furthermore, He used Khalid Ibn El-Walid as a commander of the army for his skills and military wisdom, statesmanship or statecraft as used Bilal to the Public treasury for his piety, asceticism, and good mastermind.

The standards which upon it the worker be chosen for the work or the function; it's just his ability to do this work and if he suitable for this work or not.

Employee's Ethics in Islam:

Islam came with several ethics and Muslim must commit with it at his work regardless of the job or craft type.

These ethics and Islamic principles are obligatory for every Muslim worker, whatever his work; these ethics are:

1- Strength

2- Honesty

As Allah the Highest says: {**One of the two women said: 'Father, hire him. The best who you can hire, is the strong, the honest}** (AL-QASAS, 26); and says: {he king said: 'Bring him before me. I will assign him to myself. 'And when he had **spoken with him he said: today, you are firmly established in both our favor and trust.}** (YUSUF, 54) and says in Jibril features **{It is indeed the word of an Honorable Messenger, of power, given a rank by the Owner of the Throne}** (AT-TAKWEER, 19, 20).

As all or most of the ethics fall under two importance ethics. Firstly we will discuss them then will discuss some required ethics of the employee as follows:

1- Strength

"Strength" is originally against the "Weak", also known as a source of activity, growth, and movement. It also divided into natural, vitality, and mentality. As the strength in the work means the ability to make this work (Almaany dictionary, www.almanny.com) and the Quran used the "Strength" as determined sincere and stiffness, as Allah says **{And when We made a covenant with you and raised the Mount above you, (saying) 'Take what We have given you forcefully and remember what is in it, so that you will be cautious}** (AL-BAQARAH). That means we must love and take care of our works, and work hard without inclining to the weakness or fatigue (Sharabasi, 1987, P.249).

Strength means the efficiency to complete the required work, as the strength is related to the capacity. In this purpose (Ibn Taymiyyah, D.T) said: strength in the war comes from the courageous heart, the experience of war, and fighting types but the strength of judge between people comes from the knowledge of justice which is indicated by the Quran, Sunnah, and the capacity to implement the provisions between them.

As (Humaidan, 1429) says: the strength of the functional ethics is the first qualification to take over any position or function, as Allah say: **{One of the two women said: 'Father, hire him. The best who you can hire, is the strong, the honest}** (AL-QASAS, 26). Also, the Prophet -PBUH-praised the strong believer as he says: **{A believer who is strong (and healthy) is better and dearer to Allah than the weak believer}** (Narrated by Muslim, 2664).

The strength of the believer is required to the function and other things. Allah ordered the Prophets for this purpose when said: **{we inscribed for him upon the Tablets all kinds of exhortation and clear explanations of all things. So take it forcefully, and order your nation to take what is best of it. I shall show you the home of the wicked.}** (Al A'raf, 145) and said: **{We said): 'O John, hold fast to the Book', and we bestowed on him judgment while yet a child}** "(Mariam, 12). Also Allah ordered the believers to have the strength: **{And when We made a covenant with you and raised the Mount above you, (saying) 'Take what We have** given you forcefully and remember what is in it, so that you will be cautious} (AL-BAQARAH, 63) and said: {Muster against them whatever you are able of force and tethers (ropes) of horses, so that you strike terror into the enemies of Allah and your enemy, and others besides them whom you do not know but Allah does. All that you spend in the Way of Allah shall be repaid to you. You shall not be wronged.} (AL-ANFAL, 61).

(Hamdan, 1429 A. H) explains that the strength of the employees is included in two types: physical and spiritual strength.

Physical strength is the ability to do the function and there is nothing preventing you from doing your work.

The spiritual strength means the practical strength which makes you be able to exploit the capacities, abilities, and continuing to develop and renew yourself.

(Al- Kawosi, D.T) asserts that Muslim worker has to be characterized with a sensual and spiritual strength to be qualified to perform his work. That's will be by taking all acceptable means and methods which make him stronger in his body, ready to practice his work and possessing a good and highly knowledge. The strength also helps the personal to recognize the requirements of his work to achieve the maximum services for the beneficiaries of this work. As the description of the Prophet, Mussa is {is the strong, the honest} (AL-QASAS, 26) which comes on the daughter words of the good man.

Strength includes a lot of employee Muslims ethics such as:

1- Excelling the work: perform the work in its perfect manner not only the minimum way as The Prophet Mohamed-PBUH- says: {Allah will be pleased with those who try to do their works in a perfect way} (Narrated by Al- Bihiki, Faid Al- Kader, No. 1861, part 2). The prophet-PBUH- also says: {May Allah show mercy to a man who excelled his work or craft} (Narrated by Saeed Al-Khudri, Gama Al- Osool, No. 8719). The prophet also says: {The best of deeds is that which is beneficial}(Narrated by Al- Tabarani and Ibn Asakr, Kachf El- Khafaa, No. 122). The meaning of excelling is the scientific and practical power which is considered as one of the benevolent worker's features as Allah says: {One of the two women said: 'Father, hire him the best who you can hire, is strong, the honest.} (AL-QASAS, 26).

2- Availability of the efficiency and competence for the job: as Allah says on the daughter words of the good man {One of the two women said: 'Father, hire him the best who you can hire, is strong, the honest.} (AL-QASAS, 26). She expressed and said {is strong, the honest} referring to the efficiency to work with him to graze the cattle or livestock.

The employee who feels of weakness because a healthy or psychological problem or lack of experience, he must say his ability and not require more than his right. consequently, the administration must not give him the work that he cannot bear or do. Look for the mentioned Hadith between Abu Dharr and the Prophet Mohamed-PBUH-, when Abu Dharr requested the Prophet to assign him to rule a state but the Prophet explained that the companion is not suitable to the required strength qualification.

3- Cooperation at work: the worker must commit and keen to perform his duties and collaborates with his employees to have the brotherhood spirit in the work. That has as a positive effect on the work performance; it can help the employee to perform his work quickly, with good quantity and quality. As Allah says: **{O you who have believed, do not violate the rights of Allah or [the sanctity of] the sacred month or [neglect the marking of] the sacrificial animals and garlanding [them] or [violate the safety of] those coming to the Sacred House seeking bounty from their Lord and [His] approval. But when you come out of ihram, then [you may] hunt. And do not let the hatred of a people for having obstructed you from al-Masjid al-Haram lead you to transgress. And cooperate in righteousness and piety, but do not cooperate in sin and aggression. And fear Allah ; indeed, Allah is severe in penalty. }** (AL MA'IDA, 2).

The teamwork has a good effect on improving the performance and the collective opinion is better than the individual ones. Allah the Highest says: **{And hold fast to the Bond of Allah, together, and do not scatter. Remember the Favor of Allah bestowed upon you when you were enemies, and how He united your hearts so that by His Favor you became brothers. And how He saved you from the Pit of Fire when you were on the brink of it. And so Allah makes plain to you His verses, in order that you will be guided.}** (AL 'IMRAN, 103).

Islam does not ignore the effect of the group and teamwork on the quality and workmanship which helps the nation's interests to be performed in its perfect manner. From this point; the employee has to cooperate with his colleague at the work, as Allah ordered us, according to his sensory or physical strength which he has to use it to help his colleague and not treat him in a bad manner. In this purpose Prophet Mohamed-PBUH- says:{A believer is for a believer as a structure, each supporting the other' (Narrated by At- Tirmidhi, Al- Shikhan, and Al- Nisai by Anas, Gama Al- Osool No. 4796).

4- Coupling the work with science and knowledge: If the employee chose a particular function he should learn the related science of it to excel this work. Furthermore; he has to learn or know his work way beside it's related transactions to know the permitted and prohibited things and to avoid what harms him which is not please Allah as (AL- Ghazali) says: (Know that the collection of this knowledge must be done by every learner' (AL- Ghazali, D.T, Part 2, P. 64).

So the employee must know what is his work, how does he work, and why does he work?. In fact, the employee is responsible for knowing that as Omar Ibn Abdul Aziz (May Allah be pleased with him) said: (who works without knowing the full knowledge of the work, the bad things become more than the good things in his work) (Ibn Taymiyyah, 1983, P. 81).

The earlier Muslims unanimously narrated that the obligated man must not make anything without knowing what Allah sad about it. So who sells thing has to know Allah rules in selling. The lesser has to know and learn Allah rule in the lease. Also, the borrower has to know Allah rules in the lease. As the prayer has to know and learns the rules of Allah in this pray (Almazyed, 1403 A.H).

This is included in the administrative work and the employee has to learn and know all things about his function to perform it in the required manner, either through the regulations, instructions, training or asking an experienced man in the workplace for any ignorance related to his work.

2- Honesty (Trust):

(Yaljehin, 2002) identified the honesty as (all assignments or duties which must be done by the person for Allah and the people according to the availability of freedom and ability) (P. 336). In this purpose, Allah the highest says: **{Believers, do not betray Allah and the Messenger, nor knowingly betray your trust}** (AL-ANFAL, 27). (Ibn Kathir, 1987) said about that; the honesty is (the works which Allah trust of the man to perform it perfectly) (P. 313). (Al- Razi, 1988) said for this purpose: (after reviewing the different opinions in the trusts, the previous verse refers to the duties and assignments or duties must be done without any defection).as Allah says in several verses, such as: **{If you are upon a journey and a scribe cannot be found, then let pledges be taken. If any of you trusts another let the trusted deliver his trust, and let him fear Allah his Lord.}** (AL-BAQARAH, 283) and says: **{Allah orders you all to hand back trusts to their owners, and when you judge between people you judge with justice}** (AN-NISA', 58); and says **{(Those) who keep their trusts and their covenant,}** (AL MA'ARIJ, 32). Islam orders us to keen of the trusts because the whole people businesses and matters can't be settled and be improved without the honesty and trust in performing it.

The honesty includes that, the employee has to invest his time in good things, and perform his work its perfect manner. Furthermore, he has to perform all his duties or responsibilities toward the people and nation.

The Prophet Mohamed-PBUH- negated the faith for who is not a trustee or honest when he said: **{No faith for who is not honest or trustee}** (Narrated by Ahmed in his Musnad, 3\251, and Al- bihiki in Al-Sunan al kubra (6\ 288). That refers to the relevance of trust and faith in the existence of Allah (monotheism). In this purpose; (Ibn Taymiyyah, D.T) asserted of this relevance by saying that **{the trust comes from the fear of Allah` and ignoring the fear of the human, and do not sell Allah verses for a little price'}**

(Al-Hamdan, 1429 A.H) says that: (The honesty is one of the Messengers and Prophets merits (Peace be upon them). All Prophets Nûh, Hood, Salih, Lot, and Shu'aib (Peace be upon them) said to their nation that **{I am for you an honest Messenger,}** (ASH-SHURA, 107). Delivering the message needs to the highest level of honesty as the Prophet Mohamed was known as the honest before the prophecy and after it, he executed the honest as it must execute.

Honesty is one of the important ethics that must be held by the Muslim employee. for the heaviness of the honesty, the earth, and the mountains refused to bear it cause of its value and how it is too hard; but the human carried it as Allah the Highest says: **{We offered the trust to the heavens, and the earth, and the mountains, but they refused to bear it and were afraid of it, and the human carried it. Surely, he is a harmdoer, and ignorant.}** (AL-AHZAB, 72).

Honesty means that the employee can't is tergiversator, cant breaking the promises and lie. As Allah says **{Believers, do not betray Allah and the Messenger, nor knowingly betray your trust}** (AL-ANFAL, 27). The Prophet Mohamed-PBUH- said, **{There are three signs of a hypocrite: when he speaks, he tells lies; when he makes a promise, he breaks it; and when he is entrusted, he betrays his trust}** (Agreed upon this Hadith by Abu Hurairah).

The honesty for the employee includes his feelings of the enjoyment of his work and he has to know that he is responsible for his works and deeds toward Allah; as the Prophet Mohamed -PBUH- says: **{All of you are guardians and are responsible for your ward}** (Sahih Al-Bukhari, 893 and Sahih At- Tirmidhi, 1705).

When someone (employee) has the strength and honesty; it helps him to perform his work in its perfect manner and makes him be qualified more than the others even if he have little power and honesty as (Ibn Taymiyyah, D.T) said.

<u>The honesty features include several ethics of the Muslim employee, such as:</u>

1- Security at the work:

Al- Gozeh definite the "Sincerity" as clearing the work from any aims to the self which means the work has to be away from the individual needs. (Abu Dhf and Al- Waste, 2007).

Allah the Highest says: **{Yet they were ordered to worship Allah alone, making the Religion His sincerely, upright, and to establish their prayers and to pay the obligatory charity. That is indeed the Religion of Straightness}** (AL-BAYYINA, 5). The Prophet Mohamed-PBUH- says: **{Fear Allah wherever you are, do good deeds after doing bad ones, the former will wipe out the latter, and behave decently towards people}** (Narrated by At- Tirmidhi, Albr book, 1987, P.4).

The Muslims employees have to do the required work in its perfect manner and he has to make this work in this manner for Allah. The sincerity in the work performance increases the employee's faith. it also increases the employee will to work. All these points add another concept to the work in Islam which is proficiency and quality; that lead the employee perform his work in a good way and increase his faith of Allah.

The sincerity in the work represents on the employee in several ways, such as:

- Discipline at work: the employee keens of his work time and invests his time to make his entire required function without wasting time in any other things which are not related to his work. The employee has to care about to people rights (Reviewers, directors, colleagues, and employees). So may there is nothing worse than the betrayer man who takes the people affairs than wasting it.

He needs to make his intention to Allah at the work and know that any moment he delays or he does not execute all of his duties as required all of that mean he is taking forbidden monies. The Prophet Mohamed-PBUH- says: **{Keep your eating and drinking comes from good deeds then your supplication are answered}** (Abdul Allah Ibn Abbas, Targhib - Al- Tarhib, 3\17).

The Muslim employee must not exploit his position at work for self- interest, his relationships, friendship, to take the public money by unacceptable way, spending more than the particular money to him or taking illegal gifts and bribery to make a service for the briber or anyone else, all of that are called (Administrative Corruption or deviation).

The Prophet Mohamed says: **{When we appoint someone to an administrative post and provide him with an allowance, anything he takes beyond that is unfaithful dealing}** (Narrated by Abu Dawoud, Al-GhRAG- AL Emarah- Al- ghae book, 2943). the prophet -PBUH-appointed a man from AL-azd to collect the charity (Sadaqa) and when he came to the Prophet Mohamed told him that {This is for you and this has been presented to me as a gift" then the Prophet Mohamed said " What about an employee whom we employ and then he comes and says, 'This amount (of Zakat) is for you, and this (Amount) was given to me as a present'? Why didn't he stay at the house of his father and mother to see if he would be given presents or not?" and said," When we appoint someone to an administrative post and provide him with an allowance, anything he takes beyond that is unfaithful dealing.} (Means betrayal) (Narrated by Al-Bukhari in his Sahih, part 13, 7197). Abdul Allah Ibn Amr said, the prophet -PBUH-{Allah's Messenger (Peace be upon him) cursed the one who bribes and the one who takes bribes} (Sunan Abu Dawoud (3580) and Musnad Ahmad 11\47).

Securing and keeping up the work secrets: Islam elicited to keep work secrets as it one Islamic ethics which leading to achieve the ambitious and keep all things in a good way as El-Madwardy says "Know that keeping the secret is one of the successful ways and manners that keeps all things in a good way" (Narrated by El-Quasi, D.T).

Keeping the Muslim employee for his secret at the work referring to his honesty and its makes him earn people trusts and wants to befriend with him. In the other way; if he Divulge secrets, people (Directors, Colleagues, Employees, and Reviewers) will hate and do not trust him as the Prophet Mohamed said {When a man narrates a narration, then he looks around, then it is a trust.} (Narrated by At- Tirmidhi, Sunan At- Tirmidhi 1959). Quran Kareem elicits us to keep our secrets to keep our promises because the secret comes from the promise as Allah says" And keep your promise. Surely, the promise will be questioned." (Al-'Isra', 34).

(Al- Kawosi, D.T) said that: who has a good patient, loyalty, self- control, and honesty will know the greatness of keeping the secret up as Ali Ibn Abi Talib says (your secret is your prisoner so if you speak you become in its prison). Omar Ibn Abdul Aziz (May Allah be pleased with him) said (Hearts is the containers of the secrets, the curing is considered it's closed, and the tongue is considered its keys so every man keeps his secret key for himself).

Keeping the work tools, devices, and instruments or use them for his work only is considered as one of the employee honesty types. Furthermore, he must not use them to his interests and his benefits to the relationships, friends or any who has any service he has with them. These tools, devices, and instruments are considered honesty toward the employee whatever his work, as the Prophet Mohamed-BPUH- said:{All of you are guardians and are responsible for your wards.} (Sahih Al-Bukhari 893, At- Tirmidhi 1705).

The Muslim employee must avoid any type of fraud and deceiving during his work as it is forbidden in Islam as the Prophet Mohamed-BPUH-said: {He who deceives is not of us} (Narrated by Ibn Hibban 1107 and Tabaraani in Al- Kabeer 10234).

Advice: The advice is a word includes the honesty and sincerity to who you advise in a morally way by saying what is good to him and materially by advising, working, and acting as the what the Prophet Mohamed-BPUH- said about the advice {Religion is sincerity, religion is sincerity (Al-Nasihah), religion is sincerity. They said; "To whom, O Messenger of Allah?" He said: "To Allah, to His Book, o His Messenger, to the imams of the Muslims and to their common folk.} (Sahih Muslim, Al- Iman book, 205). The Prophet ordered us to give the advice to those who has consulted us. The Prophet is considered it (The advice) from the honesty or sincerity when he said: {He who is consulted is trustworthy.} (Narrated by Abu Dawood No. 5123, Ibn Majah (3745), and At- Tirmidhi (2474), (2977).

The advice is one of the ethics ways which is elicited by the Prophet Mohamed-PBUH- also he praised the worker that give advice and said {The best gain for the worker when he advises} (shuab El- Iman to Al- bayhaqi (1177). The advice in the professional work has to be from all of the subordinators, directors, reviewers, and clients to whom is a need for an advice. The advice is obligatory for all Muslims also the worker is responsible for the guarded work duties as the Prophet-PBUH- said to his companions that {heard Messenger of Allah-PBUH- saying, "All of you are guardians and are responsible for your wards. The ruler is a guardian and responsible for his subjects; the man is a guardian and responsible for his family; the woman is a guardian and is responsible for her husband's house and his offspring, and so all of you are guardians and are responsible for your wards. } (Al-Bukhari and Muslim, Book 1, Hadith 653)

1- Justice

Justice is to give everyone his right without exaggeration or negligence; it's said that: giving the rights with equality among the beneficiaries. (Al- Hamadan, 1429 A.H).

Justice (Equality) is ordered by Allah to be applied among people in rights and duties; Allah the Highest says: {Allah orders justice, and good deeds, and giving to one's kindred. He forbids indecency, dishonor and insolence. He admonishes you in order that you take heed} (An-Nahl-90) And Allah the Highest say: {My Lord ordered justice} (Al 'A'raf- 29); Allah the Highest says: {Do not touch the wealth of the orphan, except in the fairer manner until he reaches maturity. Give just weight and full measure} (AL-'AN'AM-152); Allah the Highest says: **{But if you judge, judge between them with fairness. Allah loves the just.}** (AL MA'IDA-42), Allah the Highest says in -Hadith Qudsi-: **{O MY servants! I have forbidden (injustice) for myself, and I have made it forbidden amongst you, so do not oppress one another}** (Narrated by Muslim, the book of Righteousness and Maintaining Good Relations with Relatives, 2577, 1393 A.H).

For such reason, the worker should take care of the absence of justice, as the consequences of injustice is so grave in this world and the hereafter, Allah the highest forbidden the injustice because of its grave subsequences, and the prophet Mohamed-PBUH- says: **{Beware of the supplication of the oppressed because it rises to the heaven as if it is a spark}** (Sahih Al-Jami, 118). the prophet Mohamed-PBUH- says: {Beware **of the supplication of the oppressed; for indeed there is no barrier between it and Allah}** (Sahih al-Bukhari, 2448), and the prophet-PBUH- says: **{There are three whose supplication is not rejected: The fasting person when he breaks his fast, the just leader, and the supplication of the oppressed person; Allah raises it up above the clouds and opens the gates of heaven to it. And the Lord says: 'By My might, I shall surely aid you, even if it should be after a while}** (Al-Suyuti, Al Jami Al Saghir, 3520).

So the unjust employee doesn't think that this negligence of his punishment is an acknowledgment of his act; but in fact, it is negligence for affliction, for this purpose the prophet-PBUH- says: **{Allah will let the wrongdoer carry on until, when He does seize him, He will never let him go}** (Sahih Muslim, 2583). Justice is a necessary requirement for Muslim employee's behavior in his interactions with the others; as he is entrusted with this work, so he shouldn't be affected by relationship, friendship, or conflict, as the prophet-PBUH- says about the urge on justice when having the power:

{Behold! the Dispensers of justice will be seated on the pulpits of light beside God, on the right side of the Merciful, Exalted and Glorious. Either side of the Being is the right side both being equally mrneritorious. (The Dispensers of justice are) those who do justice in their rules, in matters relating to their families and in all that they undertake to do} (Sahih Muslim, No. 1207), the prophet-PBUH- also says: **{None is ruling ten of people but he is brought cuffed, in the day of the resurrection, until the justice releases him or the injustice degrades him}** (Sahih Al Jami Al Sagheer, 5571).

Furthermore, the prophet-PBUH- confirm the importance and the necessity of justice (Ibn Taimea, D.T, 91) and- Ibn Taimea- says that; people affairs will be achieved in this world by applying justice, so it is said that: Allah establishes the fair state even if it is a state of disbelievers, and not establish the unfair state even it is a state of believers, and it is said that: this world lasts with the justice and disbelieving, but not lasts with the injustice and Al-Islam. (Al Qassemy, 1977 A.B) mention that Omar Ibn Abd Alaziz when he asked and said that: (Guide me for a man from Egypt who has honor and righteousness to let him assume its prayer! It is said to him that: there are two men; Muaawia Ibn Abd Al-Rahman Ibn Muaawia Ibn Hadig, and Ayoub Ibn Sharhabeel, then Omar said: which is more justice than the other? They said: Ayoub, Omar said: I want this man).

According to this meaning, Omar Ibn Abd Alaziz chose the man who is more justice the other to give him the reign. In fact, employee justice is divided into two sections:

A- Justice with himself by carrying it on the interests and forbidding it from behaving badly.

B- Justice with others which consists of three levels:

1- Employee justice with those who are less than him: like director justice with his employees.

2- Employee justice with those who are higher than him: like employee justice with his directors.

3- Employee justice with those who are equal to him: like justice with his coworkers.

If the employee is fair with his co-workers, directors, and the employees under his control; then the works will be performed in accordance with wisdom methods, achieve its greatest gains, and these works will be flourished and developed. In contrast, if the justice replaced with injustice, then every one of those will envy on the other and for sure this not well in the work, the work performance will continue as we want and Allah the Glorified wants. Consequently, the work will be achieved by justice and acceptance of what Allah gives of money and posts. By justice, souls calm down and hearts relieve. The performance of the works should be based on justice, and this is the essence of being an employee. As justice being the essence of the employee work it's reflecting his heart and intention righteous, the employee also must deal with people in his work filed by justice. As we mentioned before, the employee can patronage someone upon the other because of friendship or nationality, but only works according to what makes Allah be pleased, and doesn't prefer someone with a certain service or work.

The justice is the basis of governance as (Al Mawardy) mentioned, justice must be achieved in order to avoid injustice which leads to displeasure; that means the work will not be achieved. In fact, injustice has various forms in the work:

♦ Monopolization: messenger of Allah-PBUH- says: **{Anyone monopolizes food, he is wrong}** (Sahih Muslim, narration No. 2, part 3). Islam has forbidden the monopolization and considers it as a crime because it's one of greediness and selfishness forms. In fact, there is an immaterial monopolization; such as employee monopolization whatever the position of this employee whether a minister or a manager, whereas he thinks that he is an employee only for his family and his friends and forgets that he is an employee for everyone. Consequently, this is considered as injustice and will only end by justice.

♦ Cheat: Messenger of Allah-PBUH-says: **{Who cheats us is none of us}**, (Ibn Hian authentication, 1107, and al tabarani al kabeer lexicon). Cheat is one of injustice forms which end only by justice.

2-Truth:

The truth is saying the reality and the talk came in accordance with the fact. The truth is ordered by Allah Glorified, Allah the Highest says: **{O you who have believed, fear Allah and be with those who are true}** (AT-TAWBAH, 119) the truth is one of the characters of righteous people. Allah the Glorified promise the truthful people with paradise; Allah the Highest says: **{Indeed, the Muslim men and Muslim women, the believing men and believing women, the obedient men and obedient women, the truthful men and truthful women, the patient men and patient women, the humble men and humble women, the charitable men and charitable women, the fasting men and fasting women, the men who guard their private parts and the women who do so, and the men who remember Allah often and the women who do so- for them Allah has prepared forgiveness and a great reward}** (Al-Ahzab, 35); Allah the Highest says: **{Obedience and good words. And when the matter [of fighting] was determined, if they had been true to Allah, it would have been better for them}** (Muhammad, 21), Ibn Mas'ud (may Allah be pleased with him) said that: Messenger of Allah said: **{Hold on to truth, for being truthful leads to righteousness, and righteousness leads to Paradise. Verily, a man will keep saying the truth and strive for truth, until he is written before Allah as very truthful}** (Sahih Muslim, 2607). Employee's truth gives him the quietism in his work, and it is the essence of sincerity in work performance. The employee performs his work perfectly and depends on Allah in all his affairs. Employee truth means that a clear truth about certain information transferred from one person to another inside the administrative authority. The truth is a protection from Suspicion and it is a good deed aims to the pleasure of Allah. (Al-Ghazali, D.T) says about Muslim ethics: "the honest work is the one where there is no cheating in it, as it stems from sincerity, and it doesn't have any deviation because it stems from faith). It is said that: the most sincere words that are said truthfully and affect their hearer. Allah praises many of his prophets with truth; Allah the highest says about his prophet Abraham-PBUH-: **{And mention in the Book [the story of] Abraham. Indeed, he was a man of truth and a prophet}** (Maryam, 41), and Allah the highest says about Ishmael-PBUH-: **{And mention in the Book, Ishmael. Indeed, he was true to his promise, and he was a messenger and a prophet}** (Maryam, 54); Allah the Highest say about Joseph-PBUH-: [He said], **{Joseph, O man of truth, explain to us about seven fat cows eaten by seven [that were] lean, and seven green spikes [of grain] and others [that were] dry- that I may return to the people; perhaps they will know [about you}** (Yusuf,46); Allah the highest says about Idrees-PBUH-: **{And mention in the Book, Idrees. Indeed, he was a man of truth and a prophet}** (Maryam, 56).

Employee truth types:

The employee is honest with Allah, people (Auditors "Beneficiaries", Coworkers, Directors) and honest with himself.

- **Truth with Allah**: it will be by performing all the works in sincerity for the sake of Allah. It should be clear of Pretension and repute. If anyone performs any work without the intention of sincerity for the sake of Allah, Allah doesn't accept any of those works. Muslim acts sincerity while performing all religious duties; by giving it its right and performing it in an ideal way.

- **Truth with people** (Auditors "Beneficiaries", Coworkers, Directors): Employee shouldn't lie on them. The employee should act honestly while performing his work with them. Prophet Mohamed-PBUH-: says: **{It is great treachery that you should tell your brother something and have him believe you when you are lying}** (Abu Dawud, Sunan Abi Dawud, 4971).

- **Truth with soul:** Truthful Muslim employee doesn't cheat himself and knows his defects and faults and rectifies them if he faults in a certain performance and none knew that fault; truth makes him rectifies this fault. Consequently, his performance is improved by the sincerity of Allah and the sincerity of his intention, Allah the highest says: **{He who does evil or wrongs himself and then asks forgiveness of Allah will find that Allah is the Forgiver, the Most Merciful.}** (An-Nisa' 110). The truthful employee knows that the truth is the path of salvation, and the prophet Mohamed -PBUH-: says: **{Leave that which makes you doubt for that which does not make you doubt, for truth is peace of mind and falsehood is doubt}** (Sunan Al-Tirmidhi, 2518). Employee truth leads to the confidence with employees, directors, and beneficiaries (auditors). Subsequently, this means performing work in a perfect way; Allah the highest says: **{And he who comes with the truth, and confirms it, those are they who surely fear Allah}** (Al-Zumar- 33).

<u>**Truth forms of the Muslim employee:**</u>

* <u>**Personal integrity**</u>: Truth in the dealing with people; personal integrity creates confidence which means gaining people's highly confidence. Truth is to say reality, as we mentioned before, the words came in accordance with the facts. Integrity: have the same meaning; that is to say; in other words, the integrity is fulfilling the promises and executing the expectations. This requires from the employee an Integral character which has the harmony with itself and others.

* <u>**Truth of transaction**</u>: Employee whatever his position if he transacts with someone truthfully; no cheat, no deception, and no forgery, his performance will be perfect.

* <u>**Truth of intention**</u>: if employee intends to do what he should do it without hesitation and keeps on his work without giving attention for anything till he performs his work. The intention is the start of every success and it is the first step toward the top, as (Carlos Castino) says: "In the universe, there is a power that can't be measured or described; this power is: the intention". (Wayne W. Dyer, D.T).

Muslim employee shouldn't lie, if he called a liar he will lose people's confidence, in addition, he will lose the credibility of the others, his work, of his organization. This will cause a lot of loss for the employee and organization. For the Importance of truth and lay described as a crime for Muslim; this concept is confirmed by Safwan Ibn Selem (may Allah be pleased with him) says: **{The Messenger of Allah, may Allah bless him and grant him peace, was asked, 'Can the mumin be a coward?' He said, 'Yes.' He was asked, 'Can the mumin be a miser?' He said, 'Yes.' He was asked, 'Can the mumin be a liar?' He said, 'No.}** (Al-Albany, Daaif At targheeb, 1732, and Ibn Higr Al Askalany, authentication of Mushkat Al Msabih 4\389).

From what we have mentioned before; it clarifies the importance of this magnificent character in work performance. The truth is a good deal for the employee in both the world and the hereafter, as he gains the reward from Allah and he also gains the confidence of his clients, his employees, and his directors. We can see how wonderful the Saying of Ibn Abas (May Allah please him): (There are four moral characters: truth, shyness, good manner and gratefulness. and who has them is a winner) and Al Shoaby says: (You should be truth; whereas you thinks that truth harms you, it actually serves you. you should avoid lying whereas you thinks that it serves you, it actually harms you) and Abd Al Malek Ibn Marwan said to the teacher of his children: (Teach them the truth as you teach them Al Quran).

3- Tolerance and good treatment:

Tolerance is dealing with the others with Facilitation and easiness in word and deed.

Islam urges on tolerance with all people; tolerance is a noble moral manner, and Muslim employee should be characterized with it while performing his work. Allah the highest says: **{Tell the believers to forgive those who do not look for the Days of Allah, so that He recompenses the people for what they have earned}** (Al-Jathiah- 14).

Tolerance is something good in Muslim's soul like generosity and munificence. Tolerance represents the ecstasize of the heart, the flexibility in treating between people, cheerfulness in the face by openness and happiness, Truth in the dealing without any cheating.

Tolerance has many forms and types:

- Meet people with cheerfulness and happiness.
- Start with greeting and salutation.
- Being polite and talk in a good manner.
- Cheerfulness
- Forgiving the gaffes and slips.
- The goodness of companionship.

This moral character is one of the best deeds. Prophet Mohamed-PBUH- says: **{One of the characteristics of good faith is: the patience and the tolerance}** in fact the whole religion with all its deeds is tolerance and easiness, Allah the Highest say: **{Indeed, as-Safa and al-Marwah are among the symbols of Allah. So whoever makes Hajj to the House or performs 'umrah- there is no blame upon him for walking between them. And whoever volunteers good- then indeed, Allah is appreciative and Knowing}** (AL-Baqarah, 158) and our prophet -PBUH- was asked: {which religion does Allah Almighty love the most? He replied, the simple Hanifiyya one.} (Al-Albani- Book 14, Hadith 287).

The employee should be characterized with forms and types of this tolerance with those he knows and those he doesn't know, Allah the Highest says: And **{[recall] when We took the covenant from the Children of Israel, [enjoining upon them], "Do not worship except Allah; and to parents do good and to relatives, orphans, and the needy. And speak to people good [words] and establish prayer and give Zakah." Then you turned away, except a few of you,** and you were refusing} (Al-Baqarah, 83), and the messenger of Allah -PBUH- says: {You must be compassionate. Whenever there is compassion in something, it adorns it, and whenever it is removed from something it disgraces it} (narrated by Muslim in the Righteousness book, the section of compassion, 2165).

One of the ethics of the prophet -PBUH-; the softness and tenderheartedness, as these are on of tolerance forms. In this purpose; Allah the Glorified Prescribed his prophet- PBUH- with this: {So by mercy from Allah, [O Muhammad], you were lenient with them. And if you had been rude [in speech] and harsh in heart, they would have disbanded from about you. So pardon them and ask forgiveness for them and consult them in the matter. And when you have decided, then rely upon Allah. Indeed, Allah loves those who rely [Upon Him]} (Ali 'Imran, 159). Islam urges on tolerance in work; because of its positive effect upon the people life. Islam Prescribed the tolerant man in selling, purchasing and in the time when he takes his money from debtors as one of the best believers. the prophet Mohamed -PBUH- asked the mercy for the man who characterized with tolerance in his dealings, as the prophet -PBUH- said:{May Allah show mercy to a man who adopts a kind attitude when he sells, buys and demands for the repayment of loans} (Narrated by al-Bukhari, Sahih al-Bukhari, 2076).

Tolerance is one of Islamic Religious Law requests; it also plays a great role in dealing easiness among people and in achieving works, so the prophet-PBUH- prayed for everyone is took over an affair of his nation affairs, and he was compassionate with the nation, as The Messenger-PBUH- said: {O Allah! Treat harshly those who rule over my Ummah with harshness and treat gently those who rule over my Ummah with gentleness} (Muslim, Sahih Muslim, 1828). By this tolerance, life becomes easy. From this point; it is required from Muslim employee to treat other people well whatever they are; whether directors, employees or clients.

Good treatment (sociability): is a social duty (Al-Hamdan, 1429), Allah the Highest says: {And [recall] when We took the covenant from the Children of Israel, [enjoining upon them], "Do not worship except Allah; and to parents do good and to relatives, orphans, and the needy. And speak to people good [words] and establish prayer and give zakah." Then you turned away, except a few of you, and you were refusing} (Al-Baqarah, 83). The prophet Mohamed-PBUH- says: {You (people) cannot satisfy people with your wealth, but satisfy them with your cheerful faces and good morals)) (Narrated by Al-Baz and Al-Hakim, 1\212, with an authentic narrating of Abu Hurairah (May Allah be pleased with him)).

The famous situation of The Messenger-PBUH- with his disbelievers' enemies after Entering Mecca, where the prophet stood in front of the **honored Kaaba** and said: {**What do you think I will do with you? They said, "Only good, O noble brother, son of a noble brother". The Prophet said Go, you are free**} (Ibn Hashim, the biography of the Prophet, 2\41). The neighbor of the prophet Mohamed was Jewish, Jews was among the population of Al-Madinah, Nonetheless the prophet treated him well till the Jewish profess Islam on the hand of the prophet Mohamed; as a consequence of good treatment and ethics of the prophet (Look for the book of disciplining the mannerliness, 7\453).

The tolerance and good treatment of Islam shows the glory of this religion and its permanent righteousness and the obligation with this religion make life easy, so Muslim employee should be tolerant and treats the clients well. The client has the right of good treatment; as they are success measurement of the organization; their impression about the organization or the authority reflect their opinion about the organization and its employees. The Muslim employee has to treat the clients by executing the following:

- Cheerfulness while meeting the clients and welcome them: Allah the Highest says: {**The ones whom the angels take in death, [being] good and pure; [the angels] will say, "Peace be upon you. Enter Paradise for what you used to do**} (An-Nahl, 32), and the prophet Mohamed-PBUH- says: {**Your smiling in the face of your brother is charity**} (narrated by At-Tirmidhi, 4\339); cheerfulness and happiness while meeting and talking them, this honored moral character is a great source of success in the work and a reason for performing your duty perfectly in the work. Allah the Highest says: {**Do not extend your eyes toward that by which We have given enjoyment to [certain] categories of the disbelievers, and do not grieve over them. And lower your wing to the believers**} (Al-Hijr, 88), and the prophet-PBUH- says: {**Do not belittle any good deed, even meeting your brother (Muslim) with a cheerful face**} (Sahih Muslim, 2626), the prophet -PBUH- also says: {**a good word is a charity**} (Ibn Haian, the Good Objectives book, 378).

- Respecting, being kindness and compassion **with** them are from the good Characteristics which are urged by Islam. The prophet Mohamed -PBUH- says: {**The Compassionate One has mercy on those who are merciful. If you show mercy to those who are on the earth, He Who is in the heaven will show mercy to you**} (narrated by at-Tirmidhi, Sunan at-Tirmidhi, 1924, part 4), and Abu Adardaa (may Allah be pleased with him) narrated that the prophet -PBUH- said:{**Whoever has been given his portion of compassion has been** given his portion of good. Whoever is denied given his portion of compassion has been denied his portion of good}** (narrated by at-Tirmidhi, Sunan at-Tirmidhi, 2013), and Hurir Ibn Abdullah narrated that the messenger of Allah -PBUH- says: **{Allah will not show mercy to a person who does not show mercy to other people}** (Al-Albani, Sahih the Solo Etiquette, 71, Hadith Sahih), and the prophet -PBUH- says: **{Allah is compassionate and loves compassion. He gives for compassion what He goes not give for harshness}** (narrated by Muslim in his Sahih, the book of Righteousness And Maintaining Good Relations With Relatives, 2592, the chapter of The Grace of The compassion).

- Presenting the available service for them, taking care of their matters, giving the consultation and advice in everything related to their transactions, and achieving their transactions quickly. For this purpose the messenger of Allah-PBUH- says: **{He who removes from a believer one of his difficulties of this world, Allah will remove one of his troubles on the Day of Resurrection; and he who finds relief for a hard-pressed person, Allah will make things easy for him on the Day of Resurrection}** (narrated by Muslim in his Sahih, the book of Full (of) Reminder, 2699). And Allah Glorified and Sublime be He in the narrative of Moses pursuit for the sake of the two women without their request says: **{So he watered [their flocks] for them; then he went back to the shade and said, "My Lord, indeed I am, for whatever good You would send down to me, in need}** (Al-Qasas, 24).

- Not Discomfiting or humiliating them, Allah the Highest say: **{And those who harm believing men and believing women for [something] other than what they have earned have certainly born upon themselves a slander and manifest sin}** (Al-Ahzab, 58). And AbduAllah Ibn Amr Ibn Alaas (may Allah be pleased with him) said: **{the Prophet was not one who was obscene, nor one who uttered obscenities}** and narrated that the messenger of Allah-PBUH- said: **{The best of you are those best in conduct}** (Sahih Muslim, 2321).

  - Bearing the harm, forgiving and excusing for their faults; usually the employee meets different categories of clients; including: literate, illiterate, old, young, light-headed, nervous, generous, and varmint, so he should carry himself to bear harm from them during performing his work, and he should be patient and forgive and excuse who acts in a way of some light-headed and foolish or who deals in a bad way. He applies this complying with the order of Allah the Highest or satisfying with the great reward of

Allah for him in the day of resurrection. Allah the Highest says: **{Who spend [in the cause of Allah] during ease and hardship and who restrain anger and who pardon the people- and Allah loves the doers of good}** (Ali 'Imran, 134), Allah Glorified and Sublime be He says: **{Take what is given freely, enjoin what is good, and turn away from the ignorant}** (Al-A'raf, 199), Allah Glorified and Sublime be He says: **{And let not those of virtue among you and wealth swear not to give [aid] to their relatives and the needy and the emigrants for the cause of Allah, and let them pardon and overlook. Would you not like that Allah should forgive you? And Allah is Forgiving and Merciful}** (An-Nur, 22), Allah Glorified and Sublime be He says: **{And not equal are the good deed and the bad. Repel [evil] by that [deed] which is better; and thereupon the one whom between you and him is enmity [will become] as though he was a devoted friend} {But none is granted it except those who are patient, and none is granted it except one having a great portion [of good]}** (Fussilat, 34-35), Allah Glorified and Sublime be He says: **{And whoever is patient and forgives - indeed, that is of the matters [requiring] determination}** (Ash-Shura, 43), and Allah Glorified and Sublime be He says: **{And We have not created the heavens and earth and that between them except in truth. And indeed, the Hour is coming; so forgive with gracious forgiveness}** (Al-Hijr, 85). In this purpose; Obiada Ibn Al Samet narrated that the messenger of Allah- PBUH- said: **{The messenger of** Allah -PBUH- **said: do you want to tell you thing with which Allah honor the edification, they said: yes, he said: be patient upon who ignores upon you, communicates with who disconnects you, gives who refuses to give you, and forgives who unjust you}** (Narrated by Al Haithamy in the conjoint of the excrescences, 8\192)

<u>Tolerance and dealing in a good manner is a necessity with the beneficiaries, as mentioned before and it also a necessity with:</u>

o The co-workers: as they have the right of the dealing in a good manner; because they are partners in the interest and advisors in the work, as (Al Hamdan, 1929) mentioned; every one of them guides the other and facilitates the function of each other, and every one of them is a mirror for the other, so dealing in good manner is a duty for each one of them toward the other coworkers, because that helps the employee to perform his work in its perfect manner. Dealing with them in goodness appears in the salutation, smile, kindness, co-operation, serving each other, advising, and overlooking the unintended shortcomings and faults.

- o   The employees: they have the right to treat them well, because they are assistants of the director and the head in their work, as (Al Hamdan, 1929) mentioned; the director can't achieve his functions without them, so the director should be an ideal for the employees in the good treatment. If the director deals with the employees in kindness, smiling, without affectation, facilitating the functions, overlooking the solecisms, truth, and justice, they will deal like this with each other and with the others. The output of this will appear in their work and their productivity. Nevertheless, this doesn't mean that the director is overlooking in applying the system and doesn't control the work and the employee's will; as this is a sign of the administration weakness. This matter is need to the wisdom and policy. The functional discipline and the perfection of the performance by the all are the essence. System applying doesn't mean cacoethes and lack of kindness in dealing and matters complication, but the system can be applied exactly with kindness, cheerfulness, goodness of treatment, and easiness, as possible. The study of (Al Omar, 1999) confirms that the modern theories started to give attention to the importance of compassion and goodness of treatment with clients and make it one of the strategies of success for organization. In addition, many of civil service systems gave attention to this matter and put regulations for it in its rules. So, the system of civil service in **Saudi Arabia** exposes, upon the public employee, the obligation of the ethics of decency and regularity bounds required in the principles of addressing with the beneficiaries, coworkers, employees, and directors without exceeding it into an insult, attack, rebellion, or defamation.

4- Patience:

The patience means self-control, tranquility, and calmness at the time of anger and skipping or delaying the revenge from anyone with the ability of its execution. Islam shows the importance of the patience, as it has a positive effect on the people in contrast with anger which makes a gap in the Muslim community. So, the patience is characteristic of prophets (Peace be upon them), Allah the Highest say: **{Indeed, Abraham was forbearing, grieving and [frequently] returning [to Allah]}** (Hud, 75), and the Saying of Allah Glorified and Sublime Be He when Allah gave Abraham good tiding of Ishmael (Peace be upon them) and said: **{So We gave him good tidings of a forbearing boy}** (As-Saffat, 101).

The patience is mentality wisdom, heart wideness, and self-control while dealing with the faults of the others in all life affairs. The patience is important and necessary moral character of employee during performing his work, and the employee should be characterized with it during his dealing in performing his work. If an employee isn't patient by his inborn character, he should carry himself out patience until he becomes far away from the anger in his dealings, and then the work's successes and develops. The prophet Mohamed-PBUH- says: **{The strong man is not the one who wrestles, but the strong man is, in fact, the one who controls himself in a fit of rage}** (Sahih al-Bukhari, 6114, Sahih Muslim, 2609).

In this way the employee can present service to the others and deals with them in calm whether they are directors, employees, or beneficiaries, deals with them in a good way, and perform his duty perfectly if he characterized with patience or tried to be patient in order to get the satisfaction of Allah the Glorified during his work. An employee may face some situations from his directors, employees, coworkers, or beneficiaries who may provoke him by criticism or opposition, whether it is in an officially meeting or an individual interview, and employee may lose his temper and provoke, or attack. For sure, this will lead to a defect in work performance in a way or another. If employee characterized with patience, he won't respond to others when they bring him gradually to be angry, consequently, he will perform his work perfectly before Allah and the others. Excluding this moral character among the characteristics of the employee, and characterizing him with it, or trying to control it, has a successful effect in performing the work in the organization.

<u>5- The obligation of the work systems:</u>

One of the good ethics which employee should be characterized with is the caring of obligation with systems, regulations, and laws of the work. As long as the employees are obligated with this systems and laws, the consequences will be reflected in the production in the work, its continuity and its development.

<u>The work obligation has many forms, among them the following:</u>

- The obligation of working hours and respecting it is among the ethics and duties of employee stated by systems and laws; respecting the official working hours, obligating with attendance and departure and not to be absent except in the case of necessity, and not to be busy during work time. The unconformity of working hours is considered as a violation of systems and regulations of work, and breaching requirements of work contract stated by the denominations of the work. Allah, the Glorified asks his slaves to fulfill the contracts when the Glorified says: **{O you who have believed, fulfill [all] contracts. Lawful for you are the animals of grazing livestock except for that which is recited to you [in this Qur'an]- hunting not being permitted while you are in the state of ihram. Indeed, Allah ordains what He intends}** (Al-Ma'idah, 1).

- obedience of directors (Officials): the obey of the employee for his directors in any field of work fields and in what serves, develops, and increases the work and increases the work productivity, Allah the Highest says: **{O you who have believed, obey Allah and obey the Messenger and those in authority among you. And if you disagree over anything, refer it to Allah and the Messenger, if you should believe in Allah and the Last Day. That is the best [way] and best in result}** (An-Nisa, 59). The employee should obey his directors' orders and the obedience should be in a fair manner even if the employee hates his director, he shouldn't mix between this and his compliance with orders in a fair manner, Anas (May Allah be pleased with him) narrated that: **{The Messenger of Allah-PBUH- said, "Hear and obey even if an Abyssinian slave whose head is like a raisin is placed in authority over you}** (Al- Bukhari, Sahih Al- Bukhari, 7142). So, obeying in a fair manner is a condition for this obeying; the worker or the employee shouldn't obey his director except in a way that Allah be blessed with and doesn't enrage Allah. The messenger of Allah-PBUH- says: **{There is no obedience to the creation, in the disobedience of the Creator}** (narrated by Ahmed in his Musnad, 1095, part2), and in this case the employee should advise his director in a good manner, as the religion is the advice. (Abu Sen, 1996) says that the obeying of the rulers is a duty for the employee, and this shows that Islam keeps the moral character of system in the Muslim community through the obeying of the rulers in what we love or what we hate, in addition to that it put limits for the abidance; this obeying doesn't have wrongdoing. Islam seeks to find the aware person who knows the limits of the obeying and doesn't exceed it to the blind obeying which leads him to the forbidden and the wrongdoings. (Al Omar, 1999 A.B) says that: the obeying in favor doesn't mean that employee can't give his point of view or doesn't be proud of his opinion, but he should express his opinion clearly and politely and without exceeding the limits of respect. Allah the Highest says: **{And [recall] when we took the covenant from the Children of Israel, [enjoining upon them], "Do not worship except Allah; and to parents do good and to relatives, orphans, and the needy. And** speak to people good [words] and establish prayer and give Zakat." Then you turned away, except a few of you, and you were refusing} (Al-Baqarah, 83).

- Co-operating in the performance; working in the spirit of the team: the co-operation among the whole Muslims upon the righteousness and goodness is a high moral character which Islam claims and urges on it. Allah the Highest say: { O you who have believed, do not violate the rights of Allah or [the sanctity of] the sacred month or [neglect the marking of] the sacrificial animals and garlanding [them] or [violate the safety of] those coming to the Sacred House seeking bounty from their Lord and [His] approval. But when you come out of ihram, then [you may] hunt. And do not let the hatred of a people for having obstructed you from al-Masjid al-Haram lead you to transgress. And cooperate in righteousness and piety, but do not cooperate in sin and aggression. And fear Allah; indeed, Allah is severe in penalty. } (Al-Ma'idah, 2). The prophet Mohamed-PBUH- says: {And Allah will aid His slave so long as he aids his brother} (Al-Albani, Sahih at-Tirmidhi, 1425).

One of the forms of employee's co-operation in performing work in a way which achieves the benefit and the good for them, Allah the Highest say: {The believing men and believing women are allies of one another. They enjoin what is right and forbid what is wrong and establish prayer and give Zakat and obey Allah and His Messenger. Those- Allah will have mercy upon them. Indeed, Allah is Exalted in Might and Wise} (At-Taubah, 71).when Dhul-qarnain wanted to build the barrier he said to the people who needed the barrier, as Allah the Highest say: {He said, "That in which my Lord has established me is better [than what you offer], but assist me with strength; I will make between you and them a dam} (Al-Kahf, 95), this means that he asked them to work with him as a teamwork in order to build the barrier. (Al Omar, 1999) says that: the work through teamwork is considered as one of the success and effective administrative methods especially in the field of the activities or services which depends on team effort such as the transactions of the bank or production of electronic machines.

6- The obligation of performing the forensic duties:

The Muslim employee should be obliged to perform his forensic duties, and due Acts of worship and at the top of it comes performing the prayers and Fasting of Ramadan. Allah the Highest say: {And strive for Allah with the striving due to Him. He has chosen you and has not placed upon you in the religion any difficulty. [It is] the religion of your father, Abraham.

Allah named you "Muslims" before [in former scriptures] and in this [revelation] that the Messenger may be a witness over you and you may be witnesses over the people. So establish prayer and give zakah and hold fast to Allah. He is your protector, and excellent is the protector, and excellent is the helper} (Al-Hajj, 78); Allah the Highest say: **{O you who have believed, decreed upon you is fasting as it was decreed upon those before you that you may become righteous}** (Al-Baqarah, 183). The performing of these duties leads the employee to avoid the prohibited works and deeds. (Al Qussey, D.T) confirms that the obligation of this moral character returns with a lot of positive and useful effects upon the worker, in performing his work; whereas gaining Allah satisfaction, achieving the tranquility, calmness, psychological stability, and the mental purity of the employee, establishing a lot of the moral values in performing the work such as: honesty, sincerity, work perfection, and creation the spirit of affection and harmony among the workers in the workplace.

<u>**Third: The Combination of Power and Honesty:**</u>

We mentioned before that The Ethics of The Function are power and honesty. All employee ethics is included in these two important moral characters. Al Quran Al Kareem combines the most two important moral characters which the employee needs, in the Saying of Allah the Glorified when Allah says: **{One of the women said, "O my father, hire him. Indeed, the best one you can hire is strong and trustworthy}** (Al-Qasas, 26). In Al Quran Al Kareem we find the combination of power and honesty in many verses, as the fallowes:

- The Saying of Allah the Glorified when He says: **{Obeyed there [in the heavens] and trustworthy}** (At-Takwir, 21).

- The Saying of Allah the Glorified about the story of the prophet Joseph when He says: **{Said [the king to the women], "What was your condition when you sought to seduce Joseph?" They said, "Perfect is Allah! We know about him no evil." The wife of al-'Azeez said, "Now the truth has become evident. It was I who sought to seduce him, and indeed, he is of the truthful}** (Yusuf, 51).

And this combination indicates the importance of combination necessity between these two moral characters, as possible. Therefore, if power and honesty are combined in a certain person, this will lead him to perform his work perfectly and he will be the most qualified with this work. Sometimes, we may not find the strong and the trustworthy and find the weak and the trustworthy, and the strong and betrayer. So, we here need to the comparison; which one is the qualified to the function? (Ibn Taimia, D.T) says: a combination of power and honesty in the people is rare, so Omar Ibn Al-Khattab (May Allah be pleased with him) says: (**O Allah, I complain to you the daring of the immoral and the inability of people of righteousness**). (Ibn Taimia, D.T) indicates that the ruling in every state; that its ruler is the most qualified person in the state; if someone is the most honest and the other is the strongest, then the more useful and less harmful than the other is the qualified for this rule. The prophet was using Khaled Ibn Al Waleed (May Allah be pleased with him) in the war since he became Muslim, the prophet says: {**Khalid is a sword that** Allah **raised upon the disbelievers**} (Narrated by Ahmed, No.43), even he sometimes made what the prophet -PBUH- prohibited, even though the prophet was presenting him for the rule of the war because he was the most qualified in this field. Also, Abu Dhar was more qualified than Khaled Ibn Al Waleed in honesty and trust, but the prophet prevented Abu Dhar from the rule and authority because the prophet found him weak. (Al Khudari, D.T) says that the best workingman who has the power of body and characterized by the honesty; the power of the body is a supporter on performing and achieving work and the honesty is the motivation which leads a worker to work well and perfectly and it is the moral character which precludes between him and cheats and negligence. Allah the Highest say: {**One of the women said, "O my father, hire him. Indeed, the best one you can hire is strong and trustworthy**} (Al-Qasas, 26). In this way, we find that all duties are excluded under these two moral characters (power and integrity) and under their combination together. If the employees obliged with the employee ethics in Islam, we can make sure of the enhancement of the performance, but also make sure of its quality and perfection, subsequently, the increasing of the productivity largely and perfectly, and the state will be one of the developed states in all fields.

The results of the employee obligation with these ethics in the function:

The obligation of these ethics has good, positive, and effective results in improvement, quality, and the development of work performance; we summarize it in the following:

- Ethics obligation leads to develop the abilities of the employees, and motivate the employees to improve the work performance.
- Ethics obligation leads to increase the organization confidence and sustain its position with its clients.
- It is the main factor in improving the efficiency of workers performance in the organization.

And it means that the organization appears in the following form:

- Control work performance away from the jobbery and the administrative deviation.
- Completing and achieving work contracts in the required way.
- Achieving high productivity and at the same time achieving interests of all parts of the work.
- The righteousness in performing works.
- Facilitating and simplifying affairs of life upon the Muslims.
- The goodness and perfection of works lead to promote and develop the Nation, achieve civilization, and transfer from the name of the developing states to the name of the developed states.

<u>We can abstract that</u>:

First: Function Ethics

Second: Employee's Ethics

The function is a lodgment
The function is a duty which the efficiency didn't be provided in it

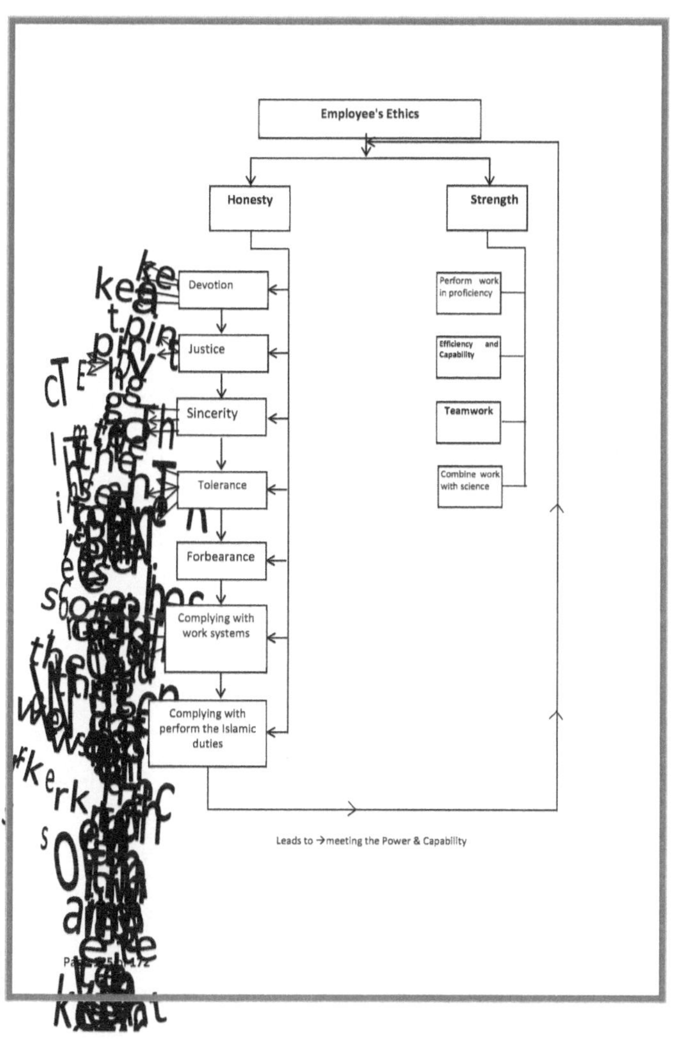

Employee's Ethics
Honesty
Strength
Devotion
Justice
Sincerity
Tolerance
Forbearance
Complying with work systems
Complying with perform the Islamic duties
Perform work in proficiency
Efficiency and Capability
Teamwork
Combine work with science
Leads to → meeting the Power & Capability

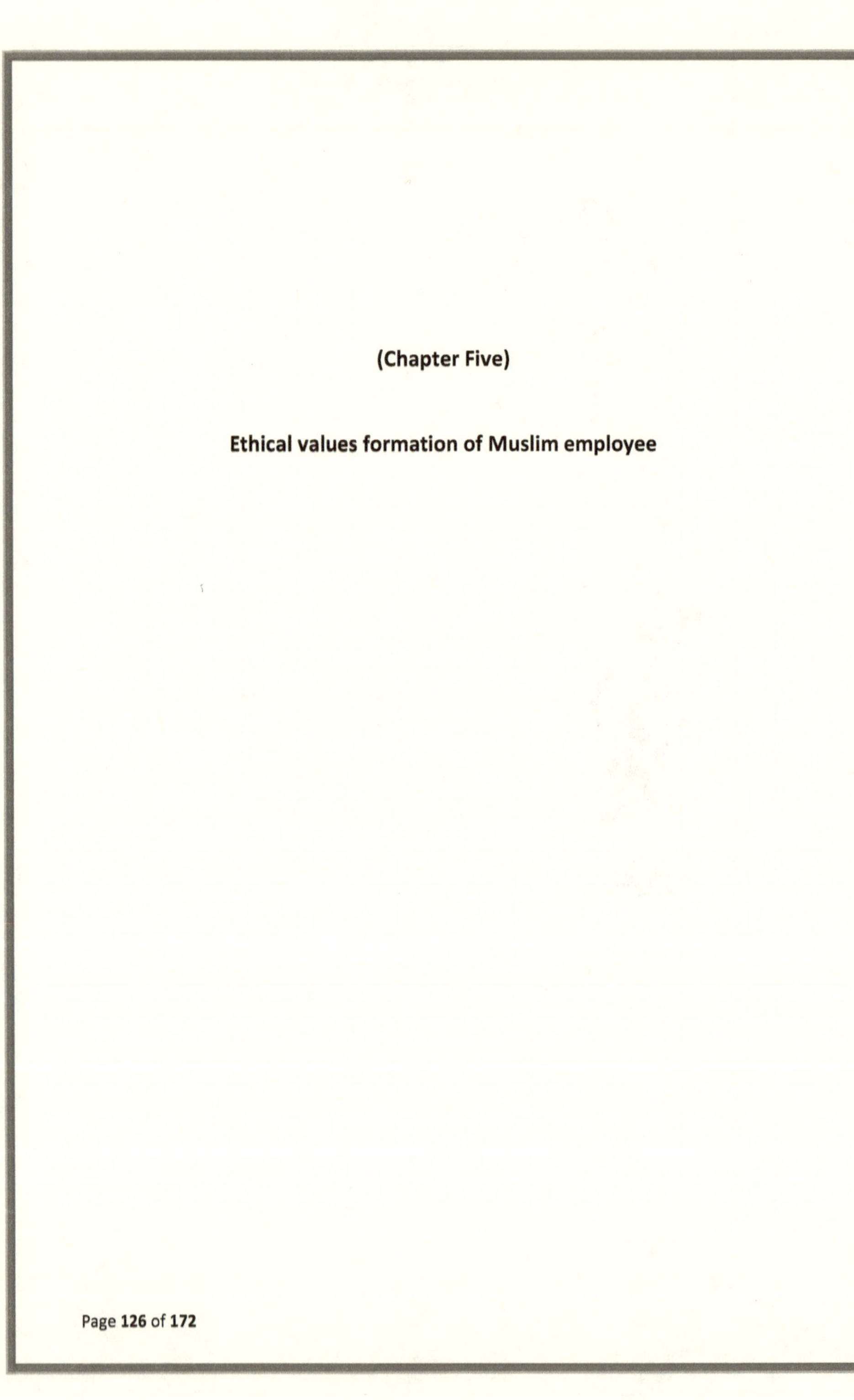

(Chapter Five)

Ethical values formation of Muslim employee

(Chapter Five)

Ethical values of Muslim employee

1- Administrative corruption in Islamic conception

2- Moral decay (Corruption in Muslim states)

3- Management audit strategy

There is no doubt that, this book here has a basic hypothesis which focuses on holding Public function; whereas this hypothesis forms the trust which the community gives it to the general employee. From this point, using this trust and keeping it is a public service which bigger than the commitment with public interests, whereas commitment rate of the general employee, whereas commitment rate is higher than any commitment rate of his **_avant- grade_ in the non-governmental sector.**

With the clear understand of this truth, situations may be raised and the employee faces ethical issues within time work, maybe a situation makes him deviates from right attitude and ethical requirements of function, and behaves in immoral ethical attitude, all these things called administrative corruption. Unfortunately, we find the deviating of a public employee from right attitude, in all societies whether developed or developing societies, it even becomes a phenomenon.

(AL- Shekhly, 2003) explains that administrative corruption in some states reached to a high level because the officials give receipts in the value of bribery which people paid it for them. The American companies offer through nationality since (1994) nearly (11) 11 billion in the international commercial agreements according to Ministry of foreign affairs in SEP 1994, and nearly trillion dollars in annual purchases market in developing states, if the bribery through nationality cost the American people their functions, it costs developing states sufficiency and assertiveness.

In spite of laws in west administrative corruption still is a phenomenon there. We should remember that they are disbelievers and they don't follow instructions of Allah, but it consider real issue in Islamic states because of corruption is not get along with our Islamic religious laws that Allah give it to us to reform world affairs and afterlife, to teach us the importance of the work according to Islamic religious laws, how to avoid corruption and related punishment. Administrative corruption in Islamic states has a lot of forms which we can't count or classify it in one legal form; like the type of crimes and its punishments in criminal law. Whereas this form of corruption is considered as a crime and mentioned in penal laws like bribery, embezzlement, detriments and earning money from the public function.

In fact, Islamic religious laws state it; the Holy Qur'an had mentioned the corruption and explained it; whereas the verb (Corrupt) and its derivatives appeared in Qur'an in fifty forms and in different denotations and many contexts. For example:

- {And when he turned away (From thee) his effort in the land is to make mischief therein and to destroy the crops and the cattle; and Allah loveth not mischief} (Al-Baqara, 205)
- {And when Moses asked for water for his people, we said: Smite with thy staff the rock. And there gushed out therefrom twelve springs (So that) each tribe knew their drinking-place. Eat and drink of that which Allah hath provided, and do not act corruptly, making mischief in the earth} (Al-Baqara, 60)
- {And [with] Pharaoh, owner of the stakes, [All of] whom oppressed within the lands, and increased therein the corruption} (Al-Fajr, 10-12)
- {Because of that, we decreed upon the Children of Israel that whoever kills a soul unless for a soul or for corruption [done] in the land- it is as if he had slain mankind entirely} (Al-ma'idah, 32)
- {Then we sent after them Moses with Our signs to Pharaoh and his establishment, but they were unjust toward them. So see how was the end of the corrupters} (Al-A'raf, 103)
- {And of them are those who believe in it and of them are those who do not believe in it. And your Lord is most knowing of the corrupters} (Yunus, 40)

Whatever, mentioned derivatives and denotation participated in one subject, all about explaining corruption, some verses which mentioned or other verses explained corruption that rustling from heads and leaders that springing corruption, verses in Qur'an participated in explaining and warning from corruption and corruptors also denying their behaviors and opinions in different manners to explain it

For example

1- {She said, "Indeed kings- when they enter a city, they ruin it and render the honored of its people humbled. And thus do they do} (An-Naml, 34)

2- {Indeed, Pharaoh exalted himself in the land and made its people into factions, oppressing a sector among them, slaughtering their [newborn] sons and keeping their females alive. Indeed, he was of the corrupters} (Al-Qasas, 4)

3- Also like a pharaoh and Karun they were corrupters by their influence, and advisers from Karun nation (People) said to him what stated in verse of the Qur'an {do not forget your share of the world. And do good as Allah has done good to you. And desire not corruption in the land. Indeed, Allah does not like corrupters} (Al-Qasas, 77)

4- {And when it is said to them, "Do not cause corruption on the earth, "they say, "We are but reformers} (Al-Baqara, 11)

5- {Who cause corruption in the land and do not amend} (Ash-Shu'ara, 152)

6- {And Moses said to his brother Aaron, "Take my place among my people, do right [by them], and do not follow the way of the corrupters"} (Al-A'raf, 142)

7- {Or should we treat those who believe and do righteous deeds like corrupters in the land? Or should We treat those who fear Allah like the wicked?} (Sad, 28)

8- {But those who break the covenant of Allah after contracting it and sever that which Allah has ordered to be joined and spread corruption on earth - for them is the curse, and they will have the worst home} (Ar-Ra'd, 25)

9- {And to those who are Jews we have prohibited that which we related to you before. And we did not wrong them [thereby], but they were wronging themselves} (An-Nahl, 118)

10- {Who break the covenant of Allah after contracting it and sever that which Allah has ordered to be joined and cause corruption on earth. It is those who are the losers} (Al-Baqarah, 27)

11- {And when he goes away, he strives throughout the land to cause corruption therein and destroy crops and animals. And Allah does not like corruption} (Al-Baqarah, 205)

12- {Allah knows the corrupter from the amender. And if Allah had willed, He could have put you in difficulty. Indeed, Allah is Exalted in Might and Wise} (Al-Baqarah, 220)

13- {And cause not corruption upon the earth after its reformation. And invoke Him in fear and aspiration. Indeed, the mercy of Allah is near to the doers of good} (Al-A'raf, 56)

14- {I ndeed, Allah does not like corrupters} (Al-Qasas, 77)

15- {So would you perhaps, if you turned away, cause corruption on earth and sever your [ties of] relationship?} (Muhammad, 22)

16- {Because of that, We decreed upon the Children of Israel that whoever kills a soul unless for a soul or for corruption [done] in the land- it is as if he had slain mankind entirely. And whoever saves one- it is as if he had saved mankind entirely} (Al-Ma'idah, 33)

17- {So why were there not among the generations before you those of enduring discrimination forbidding corruption on earth- except a few of those We saved from among them?} (Hud, 116)

From all verses mentioned, we find the following:

1- Avoiding corruption in all its different forms; can be only achieved by the following of Allah instructions and the avoiding of his prohibitions.

2- Warning believers from corrupters and hypocrite people that live among them and corrupts their life which based on Allah instructions; because of the true belief and corruption incompatible.

3- Stated in verse No. 11, {**And when he goes away**}, verse in text No. 12 about orphans affairs, verse in text No. 11 and 15 about management and people affairs, in mentioned context we discover that a very important denotation; Qur'an came to outrage the previous different cultures or which coexistence with Islam to compare between corruption expression and this type of immoral human behavior. In other words, Qur'an compared between corruption expression and immoral human behavior before all modern management theories, and states that have modern management

4- Holy verses mentioned the way of uprooting corruption in two ways or (by two methods). As (Al Kodah 2003) mentioned it.

First Method:

Strengthening the religious instinct in the believers to prevent them from corruption and fall into it.

Second Method:

Warning from the penalty of corruption as it's considered as an act against Islamic religious law when a person doesn't follow religious laws, he\ she will reserve the adequate banishment. (Under penalties prescribed by law)

From tow methods mentioned above; the advantage of Islamic religious laws appears in spiritual speech integrates into it and to elevate the soul to prevent it from corruption, and the necessity of the legal speech to classify affairs of people and states.

From this point; we can extract that great religious take care of all things and all affairs in the world, explain the immoral behaviors which come from corrupters that corrupt in the land, the religious warning us from following them because the penalty will apply on them and on their corruption. So Islamic religious put great rules if we follow these rules in life and afterlife affairs will be upright.

From the above points we can extract:

The Islamic jurisprudence is the origins of Islamic management science, as we find it with a lot of expressions and applied forms which we can through it extracting these immoral behaviors and types of managements that fall within its scope. In face; we can extract integral theory in respect of administrative corruption, resulting from this great and completed religious to resolve all issues related to corruption.

Retraction of ethical values (Corruption in Muslim states)

We know that; corruption is an old phenomenon, nearly all communities have this issue even if theses communities are modern and developed, (Mansour, 2007) said that: "The corruption is irremediable disease for these communities, it is considered as an obstructive for changing it, it also makes negative effects on the economy and the development of these communities. in regardless of what modern states issued from systems, whether these states are socialist or capitalist, this system can not prevent the administrative corruption".(AL Omar, 1999) mentioned that " France filled with administrative corruption, even this year called the year of administrative corruption". the corruption wasn't only in public companies; but also in private companies (Non-Governmental Companies). The American investment bank declared about an administrative corruption resulting from the greed of one of its employees, and he\ she has convicted with many of senior employees with administrative corruption, shortly, our goal is not to observing or comparing people but we wish to declare two important facts that (Al Gendy, 2008) refers to them:

1- Islamic community in its ancient history, when people were following the Islamic religious law, we were a great nation, administrative corruption didn't appear as a phenomena or issue because provisions of Islamic laws which overcame in communities and completely forbade the injustice, instruct people to follow Allah instructions and obliged people to follow it equally.

2- Provision of Islamic laws which addresses all issues related to work and worker affairs are separate from all other provisions that address all other human issues. Islamic laws addressed work and workers issues as it associated with other human relations, but we forget that it have to address all issues of a person because it is considered full and undivided. we also can add that civil services organizations in Islamic states need fair and clear regulations and basics, even if these organizations or states have regulations and basics; they applying it by injustice way. In fact, people forget that the Islamic religious law is the most comprehensive religion; it has a lot of spiritual provisions and directives, that build spiritual instructions into the person, to help him\ her to follow Allah instructions in work performance. Provisions of Islamic laws provide to humans great instructions for profession basic ethics, which the organizations and communities need it. Islamic religious was, still, and well guide Muslims and Humans in the field of profession ethics.

<u>But!!!!</u>

Islamic states have administrative corruption resulting from retraction of ethical values. Retraction of ethical values happening because some of Muslims ignored the provisions of Islamic religious law and other of them don't follow it. The main reason which mentioned in the chapter for a lot of reasons about administrative corruption, as (Bukhari 1429 H.A) mentioned that "Management organizations didn't apply practicing of ethics that stated in provisions of Islamic religious law".

In spite of the importance of applying ethics, a lot of studies, books and essays discussed issues of management ethics in Islamic religious law and the corruption as an issue. All books and essays ... etc reached to solves in theorizing ways, studies proved that the laws which had issued, the organizations don't apply it freely.

So in our book, we will try to put strategy and methods to apply it practically and we can solve issues and fight against administrative corruption, and support profession ethics of Muslim employee.

<u>Management Audit Strategy:</u>

From mentioned subjects we can see the importance of employee's ethics and, and the seeking of all nations to apply it and for all employees to follow it. Furthermore, these ethical values reflect the confidence of organization, its employees, and its systems, In addition to the trust of the community in these organizations. Whereas commitment with function ethics leads to develop employee's performance and consequently, it develops the performance of the organization. All mentioned factors take part in developing community.

We discussed administrative corruption, its forms, reasons, and its effects on employees, organizations, and community. In addition, we clarified the ethics and instructions which Islamic religion command it to Muslim employee to follows it. In addition to mentioned opinion of Islam from administrative corruption, and ethics that Muslims employee has to follow it in Civil services organizations and work systems. As we know there are penalties for violations, the penalty for corruption stated in all laws and work systems in all states.

In spite of all mentioned above, all communities suffering from administrative corruption and how to fight, root out or solve it?!!

As we mentioned before, some states enact laws to limit the spread of administrative corruption issues, but it still rampant, it comes back again and appears in modern or different forms. However, we understand the ethics commitments that stated in provisions of Islamic religious law are the only way and way to solve administrative corruption issue, is following Allah instructions such in era of our great Prophet Mohamed, and after him era of the Companions of the Prophet, all their issues in life solved because they followed and applied Allah instructions and provisions of our prophet Mohamed to make success, and they built a great nation .

In fact, we can see that employees work whether they work individually or in group, it suffers from administrative corruption and that's because some of them use their positions to earn personal benefits at the cost of public benefits, although laws that state enacted it. In spite of studies and researchers that tried to solve the corruption issues, but the administrative corruption still our community issue. So I tried to leave theorizing way to solve this issue, whereas previous chapters I mentioned the theoretical part to prove that we have constitutions (Provisions and Instructions) but how we can follow and apply it, or what methods of solving and fighting corruption, in order to an employee can complete his\ her work perfectly then if he do all mentioned factors, his\her role will help in developing community and this practical method is the way to use Management audit to support profession ethics in employee ethics.

Management Audit Strategy

Management Audit: It means in shortly, adjustment the performance and determines responsibility. Furthermore, monitoring and auditing the work performance to achieve a high level of performance quality. Consequently, we can reach to continuously developing in organizational performance in the community, as may be required reaching to community development, because of developing employee performance reflects on developing communities and organizations.

The Strategy (Method): This strategy means a public program has many ways and actions that we can use it to achieve our goal or goals that organization planned it. It also means the tools and ways which we can use it to support profession ethics in behaviors of the employee and execute it through ways that lead to achieving strategy's goals.

Requirements to execute management audit strategy:

<u>**First:**</u> Make an inclusive and orderly audit in all organizations for current employee's performance in order to determine goals and responsibility for every employee.

<u>**Second:**</u>

Reforming the work performance to determine the level of work performance related to work and responsibilities were determined.

From this point, we here need a reform for work performance not the evaluation of it. Whereas the evaluation is a process through it, we can determine the type of function and employee performance, plus it helps us to understand the points of strength and support them, and points of weakness and adjustment them. In addition, providing suggests which include suitable solves to avoid these weakness points. Evaluating employee's performance is the only way to understand and know their performance quality, through it; we can develop and determine function quality.

Reforming process includes the following points:

* Collecting data according to the required level of current performance to achieve goals, plus caring about providing correct feedback to employees and organizations.

* Discovering and finding points of strength and providing requital for committed employees, addition to overcoming on point of weakness.

* Developing the performance and repairing it, plus overcoming of obstacles which prevent the work performance effectiveness.

* Determine employees that have function ethics and employees not committing with it.

Whatever our goal here is not to compare or theorizing, but we aim to put method that we can use to fight the corruption, in addition to employees can perform their functions perfectly. In the light of applying this reforming plan of work performance, we will discover and find that; all affairs related to reforming process need a person who is always asking, auditing and making a decision. As we know, in the same time this employee has to commit with all his function responsibilities. In order to apply "Management audit strategy" to support employee ethics, we see that, we have to creating a management theory which we can apply it and execute it in organizations, But to execute it practically, it depends on what this theory includes, and the basis which makes it worthy, accepted, refusal and be applied by employees in work fielded. From this point, we can say that, if high management accepted this theory, it's increasing the chance of applying it; that's Because it's the only method through it, we can make decisions, follow and execute and applying it.

So, in my opinion, this theory is available to apply, and it considers the best way to support and promote employee ethics to improve their performance in the work field, the theory is (Managed with responsibility) "Managed with responsibility" means commitment with responsibility can improve the performance. Allah decides that the person is a commitment with his responsibilities performance in this life; the principals of this responsibility for the employee come from faith in God and consequently the faith of resurrection.

Foundations of management with responsibility:

* Allah the highest say: {And say, "Do [as you will], for Allah will see your deeds, and [so, will] His Messenger and the believers. And you will be returned to the Knower of the unseen and the witnessed, and He will inform you of what you used to do.} (At-Tauba, 105)

* Allah the highest say: {Blessed is He in whose hand is dominion, and He is over all things competent-\ [He] who created death and life to test you [as to] which of you is best in deed- and He is the Exalted in Might, the Forgiving–} (Al-Mulk, 1& 2)

* Allah the highest say: {so by your Lord, We will surely question them all\ About what they used to do.}

 (Al-Hijr, 92& 93)

* Allah the highest say: {And if Allah had willed, He could have made you [of] one religion, but He causes to stray whom He wills and guides whom He wills. And you will surely be questioned about what you used to do.} (An-Nahl, 93)

The Prophet Mohamed- PBUH- said {All of you are shepherds and each of you is responsible for his flock. A man is the shepherd of the people of his house and he is responsible. A woman is the shepherd of the house of her husband and she is responsible. Each of you is a shepherd and each is responsible for his flock.} (Sahih Al-Bukhari)

Definition of management with responsibility:

Management with responsibility in work\ function means that: workers have to be responsible for all their commitments, choices, decisions which resulting from their behaviors.

For sure, it is necessary to have a source to recognize this responsibility for employees (Commitments and burdens of function) to perform it. For example:

In organizations or places where worker work in it should have someone who always monitoring the commitments, choices, and decisions during employ's work performance.

Whereas management with responsibility is an integrated administrative method that focuses on the employee has to commit with his all his\ her functional duties whereas he\ she become responsible for his\ her behaviors or actions and he\ she will be accounted for behaviors and actions. Allah the highest says: {**whoever does righteousness- it is for his [own] soul, and whoever does evil [does so] against it. And your Lord is not ever unjust to [His] servants.**} (Fussilat 46)

When a person (Worker) feels that he\ she responsible for their functional duties, it makes him\ her be rushed off his feet to perform their work perfectly because of him\her responsible for their work performance, then all practices which employee or professional performs it, considered as duties and the employee should commit with it.

We can even say:

Management with responsibility means that a person (Worker) have to achieve his\ her functional commitments and burdens perfectly because it considers one of his\ her responsibility and the employee need to monitor his own performance of, in addition, following and ask the employee about it (His work performance). These monitoring and supervising are considered as the factors for achieving the commitment of an employee by using the commitment with systems, standards, and instructions of the organization.

Management must have clear standards and principles to evaluate the level of employee performance.

Management with responsibility requirements:

1- Officials have to put and determine methods which the organization follows it, or may be a goal which they see it can be achieved.

2- Clarifying and determining accomplishments that were planned for all employees and officials to participate in achieving it.

3- Determining the function and its responsibilities for all employees.

4- Organization should have authority which observes and supervises employees and their performance.

5- Choosing authority which specialized in observing employee performance, his function and the employee will be accountable to this authority.

6- Choosing standards to evaluate employee and his\ her responsibilities and burdens.

*** We can extract from all mentioned factors:**

- Management with responsibility requires determining duties and responsibilities for all employees plus organize, evaluate it and providing advice for the employee related to his work performance.

- Management with responsibility depends on the responsibility which the employee feels it in his work performance. so we can say that management with responsibility will be achieved by:

1- Directors (Leaders) have to achieve and improve the employee's performance, which they supervising it and determining the function that suitable for each employee.

2- The employee has to feel that he will be responsible for his\ her function before Allah and people

- Commitments of workers with performing their duties and responsibilities is a comprehensive responsibility for everyone in the organization starting from workers till high management; each one responsible for his duties and commitments according to their positions and functions.

Steps of applying Management with responsibility:

1- Responsible for management explains all steps, work procedures and theory that workers follow it.

2- Understanding the duties and responsibilities: make sure that all workers know their functional burdens clearly and how to perform it, whereas Process of determining duties and functional burdens is very important for workers, determining the role of these duties also important for management.

3- Every employee should discuss these responsibilities with his directors.

4- Documenting all responsibilities in points like (1.. 2.. 3..), employee and director both of them should have copies of the book which includes responsibilities, these responsibilities must be updated routinely for both parties.

5- Employee puts a detailed plan for work according to forms which management give it to him in order to observe and following his work performance,

Forms include following points:

- Duties that employee should perform it.

- Benefits and supporting which directors will give it to the employee.

- Time of auditing, following and observing work, times which through it management will be sure that the work is performed in a good manner.

WEEKLY ACHIEVEMENT REPORT TEMPLATE

Employee name	:		Department	:
Function	:		Week	:

Days	working hours	Accomplishment Function	Notes
Saturday	8 – 9		
	9 – 10		
	10 – 11		
	11 – 12		
	12 – 1		
	1 – 2		
Sunday	8 – 9		
	9 – 10		
	10 – 11		
	11 – 12		
	12 – 1		
	1 – 2		
Monday	8 – 9		
	9 – 10		
	10 – 11		
	11 – 12		
	12 – 1		
	1 – 2		
Tuesday	8 – 9		
	9 – 10		
	10 – 11		
	11 – 12		
	12 – 1		
	1 – 2		
Wednesday	8 – 9		
	9 – 10		
	10 – 11		
	11 – 12		
	12 – 1		
	1 – 2		

Date :	Employee signature :

Notes of direct superior   :

* **NOTE**: Changing working hours is according to working hours of employee.

MONTHLY ACHIEVEMENT REPORT TEMPLATE

Employee name	:					
Day :	Week :	Month :	Year :	Accomplishment Functions	Preference	Accomplishment Date :
-						
-						
-						
-						
-						
-						
-						
-						
-						
-						
-						
-						
-						
-						
-						
-						
-						

NOTES :

Employee signature:
Date   :   **Direct head signature**   :

PLANS AND AUDITING JOBS TEMPLATE

Determined duties and responsibilities	Accomplishment of duties (manner of working)

6- Direct head will supervise the employee's performance to observe their work and to see if the work performance is in the required manner or not.

Consequently: director and employee both of them know the accomplishment work, the backlogs, and reasons of backlogs. By this way, they know the last developments and issues, and the will be able to determine issues and solve it.

By this process director know all his\ her responsibilities towards employees, whether observing or supervising and how to award them by all benefits that will help them to perform their works or jobs perfectly, benefits which helping them include opinions and advice. Directors and employees should discuss with each other the ideas and new suggestions, he\ she should perform all his\ her responsibilities perfectly, adding to sincerity and honesty in his\ her works, and supreme head asks and observes employees works etc...

7- Auditing and accounting: the responsibility of the director appears here, whereas director (as an employee) performs all committed duties and provides paper of accomplishment duties to others.

* Direct manager must audit accomplishment works which his\her employees perform it, and see haw this work performed is matching the standards (time, quality of performed work). If he\she find issues or obstacles weren't solved in auditing level, should put the plan to solve issues and know reasons of it in order to not repeat the mistakes, plus reviewing backlogs and its reasons and if this reason is organizational or personal reasons.

So, directors can know the reasons of backlogs and from this point he\ she can solve this issue.

We extract from mentioned factors as following:

1- By management with responsibility, we can know what employees accomplish and his backlogs.

2- We can also know from it (Management with responsibility), what employees need for performing his work perfectly whether training or tidily developing for every employee

3- From No. 1 & 2 we find employee performing his\ her work by the way which Allah ordered us to perform the work in it (The perfect manner).

4- Management with responsibility is an administrative procedure in order to every employee performs his\ her work perfectly and commitment with function ethics, it also (The function ethics) are used to fight corruption and administrative deviation that may be resulting from the employee. By management with the responsibility we can reform the employee performance.

<u>**Methods of Management with responsibility:**</u>

• Management with responsibility depends on the establishment of all responsibilities for the employee in the organization, it means every employee in the organization, whether (Director, Employee or Colleague) is responsible before Allah and people (Directors, Colleagues and Clients... etc.) responsible for his\ her performance their duties and functional burdens. As well as the directors (Leaders) are responsible for employee's performance and promoting it by honesty and strongly way before Allah and other (Directors and Clients) in addition to observing and accounting the employee in an honest manner. All (Directors, Employees and Clients) are employees bear responsibility before Allah, high management, and community.

Management with responsibility is the main reason to achieve confidence in performance works because it depends on standards and controls which come from Islamic religious law which leads to achieving goals and the results of work performance.

• Management with responsibility is considered as the point which declares limits of responsibilities. It also helps in promoting and applying of the system inside the organization. In other words, responsibility consists of a lot of sides and participatory methods.

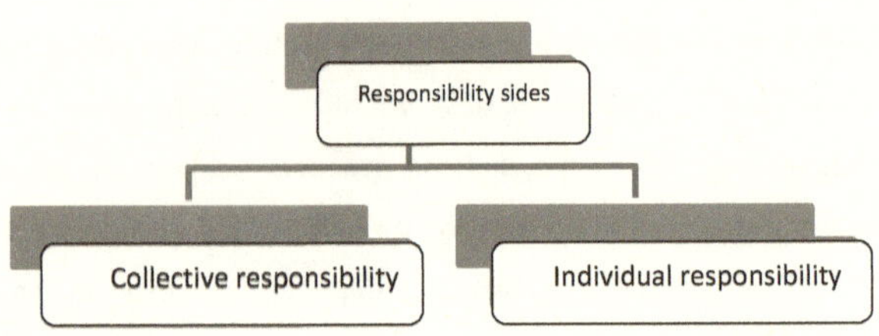

- **Individual responsibility:** it means that every employee is responsible (Director and Employee) for his\ her behavior which reflects their profession ethics.

    These responsibilities have a lot of fields; an internal field and outside field:

    - Internal field of individual responsibility:

    This means accounting any employee about accomplishment works and backlog plus his\her commitment with profession ethics which he\ she is performing it in honesty and sincerity.

    Allah the highest says: {**whether you show what is within yourselves or conceal it, Allah will bring you to account for it**} (Al-Baqarah, 284)

<u>**Outside field of individual responsibility:**</u>

This means perceived behavior of the employee whether (Actions or speech and words), and for what extent he\ she is a commitment with profession ethics.

So, internal field takes care of what is resulting in his behaviors (Actions or words), whether it's a good or bad results. Because actions, like, (Yelgin 2002) that said" The actions became like an object, it may remain more than his maker" Allah said: {**Indeed, it is We who bring the dead to life and record what they have put forth and what they left behind, and all things We have enumerated in a clear register.**} (YaSin, 12).

(Ylegin **2002**) "The human is accounted for his\ her bad actions and its effect on the others; that's well be on the Day of Resurrection. The person whose his\ her actions were bad he will be accounted for his bad actions and its effect on the people, in the same time when the person's actions are good he will be accounted for his actions and its effect on the people"

Our prophet-PBUH- said **{The one who innovates a good innovation in Islam has its reward and a reward similar to those who follow him in it-until the Day of Judgment--without lessening their reward. The one who innovates an innovation of misguidance would be sinful for it and has signed similar to those who follow him in it-until the Day of Judgment-without lessening their sins.}** (Sahih Muslim, righteousness book part1, 017)

Collective responsibility:

This means administrative responsibility for behaviors of workers (Workers\ Employees, Colleague)

And their commitment to profession ethics, we can even say that it mean the responsibility of persons before other persons.

Allah the highest said" **They used not to prevent one another from wrongdoing that they did. How wretched was that which they were doing.**" (Al-Ma'idah, 79)

This responsibility (Collective Responsibility) means that; the director is responsible for his employees and on the other hand the employee is responsible for following his director's orders.

Employee's Ethics

1- Strength (Perform work in proficiency- Efficiency- Teamwork- Combine work with science).

2- Honesty (Devotion- Justice- Sincerity- Tolerance- Forbearance- Complying with work systems).

Officials should issue decisions according to Allah instructions, he\ she also hasn't right to infringement for any of employee's rights, also he\ she hasn't right of forgiveness, he must make the decisions that include the reforming of the organization and not the benefit of one person at the expense of general benefits.

A person whose responsibility is the supervising and observing performance of employee should perform his\ her job\ work perfectly. The Prophet Mohamed-PBUH- said: **{Man's feet will not move on the Day of Resurrection before he is asked about his life, how did he consume it, his knowledge, what did he do with it, his wealth, how did he earn it and how did he dispose of it, and about his body, how did he wear it out.}** (Sunan Al Drami, introduction's book, 537) Whereas responsibility of person (Directors\ Responsibly leader) for others includes responsibility of others to reform performance of other people (Employees), The Prophet Mohamed said "**what about people where they not caring for their neighbors, and they don't know about them anything, don't given, don't instruct and don't prevent** them from act wrongs; what about people where they not learning from their neighbors, not discussing with each other, and not avoiding previous mistakes I swear by Allah, they have to take care of their neighbors or they will be banished very soon" (Al-Tbarani, Book of big dictionary as like collector of documents 5\ 459-460)

• Applying management with responsibility from high levels of management in organizations; have to perform it in its perfect manner. As the (Leaders, and Directors) commits with their responsibility; they also have to make sure that; standards of honesty and integrity are achieved in the organization.

• Everyone in the organization is responsible whether he is (Directors and Employees)

• Management with responsibility can achieve a high level of performance and promote it. Furthermore, management with responsibility develops and determines workers' performance for each employee in the organization.

• From all mentioned factors and methods of management with responsibility we can achieve what the mentioned ethical values of Muslim employee.

<u>Management advantages with responsibility:</u>

1- The confirmation of responsibility solidarity between the employers and the employees (All employees) to achieve results.

2- The commitment of an administrative method based on responsibility to execute works (All the parties of the organization comply with) which means that the employee complies with the above mentioned ethics.

3- The responsibility means that it is not fair to ask a specific person about achieving results, unless with the extent he wasted or neglected in achieving his work which means this person must be punished or rewarded according to his achievements.

4- Achieving management with responsibility and justice in the organization through the accountability of each responsible individual about the performance of his tasks as required. Consequently, there is a good management to evaluate the fulfillment of employees with more realistic and subjective basis than these ones were used annually on subjective and immune basis based on the individual characteristics and his educational background.

5- Through management responsibility, the management or the organization is able to form logical steps to collect specific and clear data about the functions and employees.

6- This management focuses on achieving the tasks and the responsibilities of each employee in a logical frame of this achievement and behaviors which helps to improve the behavior of the employees to be more commitment with the ethics of the profession.

7- Management with responsibility considers as a basic for the success of the organization as it plays a main role in maintaining the reputation and the credibility of the organization and the interests of the clients and the employees.

8- Applying the method of "Management with responsibility" by using "Strategy of The Administrative Audit" and the possibility to make it in the form of mechanisms helps in executing most of the functional strategic means to protecting the integrity and combating corruption   .

<u>National strategy for protecting integrity and combating corruption:</u>

It was decided in the meeting No. (43) Of the cabinet in (01\02\1428 A.H) the National strategy for protecting integrity and combating corruption, the means of this strategy as follows:

1- Identifying the problem of corruption in the kingdom through the following:

A- Organizing a national database for protecting integrity and combating corruption includes all the organizational and administrative documents and monitoring accurate information, data and statistics about the size and the classification of the problem, identify its types, causes, effects, priorities and its Prevalence socially, timely and spatially.

B- The specific authorities, according to its specialization, conduct periodical statistics and reports about corruption include a statement of the size, causes, types and the proposed solutions of the problem, in addition, identify the negatives and obstacles which face applying systems and procedures related to protecting integrity and combating corruption.

C- Supporting and conducting deepened researches and studies related to protecting integrity and combat corruption.

D- Availability of information for the individuals who desire to search and study, urging the specialized searches centers to conduct more searches and studies in the same field.

E- Monitoring what is published in mass media about protecting integrity and combat corruption.

F- Following up the developments of the subject locally or internationally.

2- The specific governmental authorities must protecting integrity and combating corruption through practicing its specializations and applying the related systems through the following:

A- Supply the monitoring, juridical and investigating authorities with the financial, human, experiences, practicing and techniques capabilities and adequate modern scientific means to be able to perform its tasks effectively.

B- Study the systems of the specific authorities for protecting integrity and combating corruption, administrative structures and procedures as well as regard non duality, specializations disputes between them and award them the necessary extent of administrative and financial independence.

C- The specific governmental authorities, according to its specializations, must conduct periodical revision for the systems related to combat corruption to identify the obstacles which appear through applying and study, propose suggestions to overcome those obstacles and improve the systems and field them to the specialize authority to check it and make use of the results.

D- Improve and evaluate the administrative, monitoring and financial systems to guarantee its clearness, ease of applying and its effectiveness.

E- Decreasing the procedures, facilitate, spread awareness and place them in noticeable areas so they will not lead to non organizational exceptions.

F- The officials must monitor and follow up; to make sure of the procedures work safety and if they are identical to the systems.

G- Choosing the officials in the executive administrations which are related to the public to be qualified and can treat well with supervisors, and to order the managers of administrations to end the procedures of the paperwork of people and monitor employees in order not to place obstacles before that paperwork.

H- To confirm non discrimination in treating people and not to look to the work or social position.

I- To apply the principle of the accountability of each official whatever was his position in the system.

J- To enhance the efforts of the authorities which have the juridical permit related to combat corruption.

K- To make use of the modern scientific means and the fast means of communications between the specialized governmental authorities.

L- To guarantee the clearness of the instructions related to fees, penalties, dues and its payment, to find precaution means to fill the gaps which may lead to the accessibility of corruption, including paying through banks in according with studied standards.

M- Speeding up of the decisions of corruption cases, applying the principle of indemnifying whose rights and interests have been harmed because of the corruption which will be after a final decision from the specialized court and publishing them upon the request of public attorney and the approval of the judge.

N- To work on unifying the committees of the juridical authority in a united juridical authority and award them the complete independence.

O- To confirm on the cooperation in the field of information exchange to combat corruption without breaching the banking confidentiality.

3- Adoption of clearness and transparency principle and enhance it in the organizations of the state through the following:

A- To confirm the officials that clearness is an effective mean for precaution from corruption and adopt it as an ethical mean or method which add credibility and respect to the governmental work.

B- To facilitate and raise awareness of administrative procedures, make them available for people and not to make them confidential unless the information related to sovereignty and national security.

C- Approve a protecting system for the public fund.

D- To clarify the procedures of the governmental, public organizations and limited companies' purchasing agreements and give the people, civil organizations and mass media the right to acknowledge and critic them.

E- To guarantee the freedom of exchanging information about the corruption between the people and mass media.

4- To enable the civil society organizations in protecting integrity and combating corruption through the following:

A- Enabling some representatives of those organizations to participate in the suggested National anti-corruption Commission.

B- To enable those organizations, according to its specialization, to play a role in studying the corruption phenomenon and expressing their visions and suggestions to combat it.

These means can be achieved in the business organizations and the administrative authorities by "Management with responsibility".

The principle of accountability by "Directors\ Leaders" in the organization leads to the proficiency and high quality accomplish of works. In addition, applying this method helps to show the accomplished work and helps to maintain the performance level of the employee, improve and show the weakness "Corruption or Deviation" and strength points and this exactly the management responsibility.

The most important part is to make the employee hold the full responsibility for his deeds and words and behavior "That is what the National strategy has been asserted".

- The employee "Worker" will be accounted for his deed whether he disclosed or concealed it, Allah knows it and will account him, Allah said in Quran: {**To Allah belongs whatever is in the heavens and whatever is in the earth. Whether you show what is within yourselves or conceal it, Allah will bring you to account for it. Then He will forgive whom He wills and punish whom He wills, and Allah is over all things competent.**} (Al-Baqara: 284)

- The employee "Worker" whatever its position in the work (Director, Employee or College) is responsible for his performance. Consequently, this employee will be accounted for his performance and his employees, so the Muslim employee, whatever his position, is supposed to be responsible, is committed to accept this responsibility and will be accounted for his deeds which mean that he will be committed to the profession ethics. The employee, whatever his position is considered to be responsible for fulfilling a certain duty and will be accounted for the way he fulfilled.

- The Muslim employee is required to master each devotional or behavioral deed for each deed is based on the intention of warship, Allah said in Quran:{Say, "**Indeed, my prayer, my rites of sacrifice, my living and my dying are for Allah, Lord of the worlds. No partner has He. And this I have been commanded and I am the first [among you] of the Muslims.**} (Al an'aam: 162-163)

- To master the work completely, requires commitment, honesty and devotion which require "holding responsibility".

- Achieving this responsibility will be through observation and internal following up and external observation of the Muslim employee which is called "Accountability through correcting the employee performance".

- The observation, following up, accountability, working on revealing the weakness points to correcting them, and strength points to enhance them in the performance of the employee are necessary to achieve work in proficiency; the thing which needs "Responsibility".

- **This responsibility is based on two points:**

<u>First Point:</u> the employee, whatever his position, fears Allah, Allah said in Quran

{O mankind, fear your Lord, who created you from one soul and created from it its mate and dispersed from both of them many men and women.} (Al-Nisaa:1) And fear Allah, through whom you ask one another, and the wombs. Indeed Allah is ever, over you, an Observer." The basic of this responsibility is to believe that Allah sees man, observe his deeds and will account him.

Allah said in Quran **{The Day every soul will find what it has done of good present [before it] and what it has done of evil, it will wish that between itself and that [evil] was a great distance. And Allah warns you of Himself, and Allah is Kind to [His] servants.}** (Aal-i-Imran: 30)

Allah said in Quran **{To Allah belongs whatever is in the heavens and whatever is in the earth. Whether you show what is within yourselves or conceal it, Allah will bring you to account for it. Then He will forgive whom He wills and punish whom He wills, and Allah is over all things competent.}** (Al-Baqara: 284).

<u>Second Point:</u> The others' observation for the employee performance means "The others' responsibility towards him and the organization by committing the Profession Ethics". It is considered to be necessary for human nature is not immunized against mistake and moving far from the right bath. Observation, following up and correcting mistakes is a compulsory duty for anyone who holds the responsibility to observe and follow up the performance of others, and the messenger of Allah declared that in his Hadith:**{All of you are shepherds and each of you is responsible for his flock. A man is the shepherd of the people of his house and he is responsible. A woman is the shepherd of the house of her husband and she is responsible. Each of you is a shepherd and each is responsible for**

his flock}. The director, college and high administration are all responsible for following up accomplishing of the employee and modifying any mistakes.

Conclusion

We can sum up what is explained through the entire book as follows:

- Islam declare the principle of performance and accomplishment where this occurs as (Abdelhady, 1975) asserts according to certain and identified controls and standards for individuals to comply with and they are accounted for it. Therefore, there must be controls and standards for accomplishing the balance of works and employees (Workers) perform their works in accordance with it.

I think that the strategy of auditing by using management with responsibility achieves this following up for the performance successfully and through it can adjust the performance of the employee according to their specific responsibilities, and they are conducted for them performance.

- As mentioned before, the concluded method from Islamic law is the origin of the Islamic management which is full of the concepts and examples.

Consequently, we achieved the two methods to combat corruption we mentioned before when we explained "Corruption in the Islamic Conception" which Quran mentioned as follows:

First method: Strength the religious motivation in the believer to make his faith prevent him from corruption "This can be achieved by sensing the individual responsibility, internal field"

Second method: To warn from the punishment result from corruption, as corruption is against the Islamic law and cannot be stopped; when there is no faith, unless by the suitable punishment, (This can be achieved by sensing the individual responsibility, external field), and sensing the group responsibility of others "Directors and colleges about the employee behavior" to be counted by the specified punishment by the directors and colleges. Moreover, each individual must sensor the individual responsibility in its internal and external fields by fearing of Allah and group responsibility. This can be achieved through the strategy of administrative audit by using the strategy of management with responsibility which means that each individual observes and accounts himself while there are others do the same.

- To achieve the ethics of the employee behavior and improve his performance, he needs to be observed, followed up, accounted and adjusted his performance which is called (Quality Control) and this achieved by (Administrative Audit). This strategy can be achieved by a sustained process to improve the employee behavior, performance, his commitment of the profession ethics and knowing the weakness and strength points through (Management with responsibility) for it is (The insurance of quality). It also can be achieved when the worker (Employee) sensing the responsibility either it was individually or group.

Therefore, we will heal the administrative corruption and improved the good behavior of the employee through committing with the profession ethics and having an administrative method resulted from the principles of Islam, this complete, comprehensive, great, flawless and full of religious guidelines and instructions which create in the employee a strong basis of the profession ethics.

- As a result, the profession ethics and the good behavior of the employee comes from that, Islam is discern, deed and behavior appears before us either with an external move or an internal motive for this move. To have a good and ethical behavior, the employee must commit with the characteristics of Islam (Faith and good deed, deed and intention, devotional deed, facilitate work and identify works and arrange them). Consequently, this is considered as a rule of work in Islam.

- Function Ethics
  - The Function is Honesty
  - The Function is a duty has not qualification

- Employee's Ethics is based on:

1- **Strength**: needs (Perform work in proficiency, Efficiency and Capability, Teamwork and Combine work with science).

2- **Honest**: needs to achieve (Devotion, Justice, Sincerity, Tolerance, Forbearance, Complying with work systems and Perform the Islamic duties).

The Ethics of The Employee can be achieved through combining strength and honesty.

- **To commit with Profession Ethics**: the function and the employee ethics repress corruption and prevent the administrative deviation.

- To establish these ethics in the behavior of the employee there is a need for a non-speculation execution mechanism which is the usage of the strategy of administration auditing. Such strategy led us to the need of formulate an Islamic method and apply it. This method is management with responsibility which is the base of complying with profession ethics and through it every employee can be accounted for his responsibilities and achieve the quality of the work.

Allah is the arbiter of success,,,

References

1- Imam Alhafeth Abi Alfdaa Esmail Ibn Kathir. (1987). (Quran tafser). DAR EL MAREFAH- Beirut.

2- Alwaseefy khtam Abu df. (2007), (The Quality of Education from an Islamic Perspective). The 2nd educational conference for quality, The Islamic university- Palestine.

3- Mohamed Ibn Abi Bakr Ibn Qayyim al-Jawziyyah. (D.T), (Bada'i al-Fawaid). Almohakek ala el omran. International Islamic Fiqh Academy- Jeddah.

4- Ahmed Ibn Miskawayh. (1398). (Ethics trimming and ethnic cleansing). Reviewed by ibn al-Khatib. Islamic religious Bookshop.

5- Taqy el ddein Ibn taymia. (1983). (Hisbah in the Islamic administration system). Dar al-arqam-Beirut.

6- Mohamed Ibnelrfadl Ibn Manzoor. (1993). (Arab's tongue.part4). Arab history institution-Beirut.

7- Taqy el ddein Ibn taymia. (D.T), (The legal policy to reform the ruler and people). People's publish house- Cairo.

8- Abdelmlk Ibn hashem. (1990), (the biography of the Prophet Muhammed peace be upon him). Reviewed by Amr Tedmory. Dar Elktab Al araby.

9- Ahmed Aboelhasan. (1996). (Administration in Islam). Dar el khrigy- Al-Riyadh.

10- Eman, Sofi, mariem, kwary. (2012). (Work ethics as a tool to limit from the phenomenon of administrative corruption in the developing countries). The National forum (governance of company as a mechanism to limit from the financial and administrative corruption). Mohamed Khider University, Biskra- Algeria.

11- Nader Abu Shiekha. (1981). (Administrative deviation: Analytical overview in its reasons and how to treat it). Scientific Meeting on ethical behavior in public office. Oman The Arab Organization for Administrative Sciences- League of Arab States..

12- Henri Bergson. (1971). (The origin of ethics and religion). Translated by: Samy Eldroby. Dar Al Malayin- Beirut.

13- Soltan Ibn maqsoud Bukhari. (1429 A.H). (Ethical structure for the administrative Muslim). Website of Om elqura University.

14- Abo bakr Ibrahim Altalaoa. (1995). (Theoritical basis for ethical behavior). Libya publications. Dar al kotob al watanya.

15- Anas Jaafar. (1992). (Main principles for public job in Islam and how they are applied in the kingdom of Saudi Arabia). Dar Al nahda- Cairo.

16- Hoda El gendy. (2008). (The role or religion in the public job ethics). Magazine of administrative development- issua No. (119).

17- Essam Al hmidan. (1429 A.H). (profession ethics in Islam). Alabikan library- Al-Riyadh.

18- Fawzy Hobish, (1996), (Public job and managind the employees affairs), The Arab Organization for Administrative Sciences- Oman- Jordan.

19-Anmar Haji, Mahfouz Alsawaf (D.T). (Public job ethics and their effect on performing works). Al wosol University- College of Economics and Management.

20- Khalil Al-Khudri. (D.T). (Work ethics from an Islamic perception). Om elqura University. Doctor Website.

21- Mohamed Abdelmeneam Khattab. (1402 A.H). (Memorandums about functional behavioral). Institute of Public Administration- Al-Riyadh.

22- Muhammad Abdullah Draz. (1973). (Dustoor Al-Akhalq fi Al-Qur'an). Algahreeb Abdelsabour Shahin. Al Resala Foundation. The General Presidency Of Scholarly Research and Ifta.

23- Bie Fede Doe, (1981) Public Job Ethics. Translated by Mohamed Hasnain. Scientific meeting about Ethics and Behaviors in Public Function. Oman. Arab administrative development Organization. League of Arab States.

24- Mohamed Ibn Abi Bakr El- Razi, (1988). Mokhtar El- Sahah. Lebanon library- Beirut.

25- Kamal Zaen, (1996) (Role of Social consciousness in combating Administrative Corruption and behavior and its effect on the balanced employee growth.) Arab center for security studies and training. (Training Course for Anti-Corruption)- Riyadh.

26- Mahmoud Hamdi Zakzouk, (1993) (An Introduction in Ethics Science) Edition No. (4) Dar Elfikr Elarabi. Cairo.

27- Ahmed Bettah, Ratb Al-Saud. (1996) (Extent of adherence the school directors in al- Karak province of Professional Ethics from their perspective). Dirasat Educational Sciences, Volume 23. No. (2), University of Jordan.

28- Abdullah Al- Saadan, (2005) (Affect of applying Arab applications for Public function and employee conception on public ethics.) A seminar about Values & Ethics of Public function in the modern management. Cairo.

29- Ahmed Al Shemiry, (2006) (Employee's Ethics). Edition No. (4). Al- Qassim. King Saud University.

30- Abdul kader El-Shaikhy, (2003) (The legal measures for Anti-Corruption). *Center* for Strategic Studies and Researches. International Arabic conference for Anti-Corruption. Riyadh.

31- Zohier Al-Sabagh, (1406 A.H) (Ethical Dimension in public service), Public administration magazine. No. (48). Institute of Public Administration, Riyadh.

32- Hamdi Abdelhady, (1975). (Islamic Administrative Thought). Dar Elfikr Elarabi. Cairo.

33- Fahd Al Othaimeen, (1993) (Administrative ethics in Public Function). Al *Resala* Foundation Beirut. (The message foundation in Beirut)

34- Fuad *Al-Attar,* (1972) (Administrative Ethics in Public Function). Dar-alnahda-alarabia, Cairo.

35- Mohamed Okla, (1986) (Ethical System in Islam). *Al-Risala Al-Hadithah* Library -Omman.

36- Abdurrahman Othman, (1405 A.H). (Administrative Responsibility in Context of Public Employee Ethics and Values), Public Administration: Evidences Concept: No. (43).

37- Mohamed Akl, (2001) (Behavioral Values). Arab Bureau of Education for the Gulf States- Riyadh.

38- Asar Fakhri Abd- Ellatief, (2006) (Impact of Function Ethics on Reducing Administrative Corruption in Governmental Functions). Journal of Human Sciences. No. (29).

39- Ahmed Abdel Wahab, (2000) (Organizational Behavior), Dar Al Wafaa. Al Mansoura.

40- Fouad Al-Omar, (1999) (Work Ethics and Employees behavior at Public Service and Monitoring it from Islamic Perspective), *Islamic Research and Training Institute.*

41- Abe Hammed Mohamed Al-Ghazali, (D.T). (Revival of Religious Sciences). Dar al- kotob al-ilmiyah.

42- Sabah Husain Fetehy, (2005) (*Administrative Behaviors* of *Saudi Employee* and Its Impacts on Work Ethics). Un Published *Master degree.* Faculty of Economics and Administration. King *Abdul-Aziz* University- Jeddah.

43- Ramadan Fahla, (1992) (Islamic religious Law *Treatment for Functional Deviation and Administrative Corruption).* Alfaisal magazine. No. (189)- Riyadh.

44- Adam Noah Al-Kodah, (2003) (Towards Islamic theory for Administrative Anti-Corruption and its Impacts), *Center* for Strategic Studies and Researches. International Arabic conference for Anti-Corruption. Riyadh.

45- Mafrg Al- Qusai, (D.T). (Professional *Ethics* in Islam). Manarat Library http\ www.Manaratweb.com

46- Zafer Al Qasimi, (1977) (Ruling System of Islamic History and Law). *Dar Al-Nafa'es*

47- *Ahmed* Al Mzgagi, *(1994).* (Muslim Director Ethics in Public Administration). *Magazine* of Islamic religious *Law* and Islamic Studies. Kuwait- No. (24).

48- Huda Al Mimeni, (1994) (Education to Work in Islam). Un Published *PhD degree.* Umm Al-Qura University, Faculty of Education

49- Saleh Al-Moayed. (1403 A.H). (Gain of Employees and its Impact on their behavior). El Madni Publishing House- Egypt.

50- Al Moqsqs, Mohamed, El Khrecha, Saoud, Al Mosad, Mafdi, Tachman, Ghazi (2011) (Availability of Public function Ethics in the Performances of Directors and Teachers to teach Al Badyah Al Wosta). Culture & Development Magazine. No. (42). Al-Isra University, Jordan.

51- Sobhi Mansour, (2007) (Public function Ethics and *Administrative Corruption).* Meeting of Contemporary trends to manage function, Rabat- Morocco.

52- El- Nahas Safwat, (2010) (Public function Ethics), Magazine of Administration, No.(4), Union of Administrative Development Associations.

53 Khal Al wahab, (2009) (Dimensions of Wise Behavior and it relevance to the Administrative Performance Efficiency). Arab Studies in Education & Psychology. Volume (8), No. (3).

54- Mansour Al Yousef, (1431 A.H) (Public function is Rights and Duties), *Electronic Knowledge Journal. No. (179),* http\ www.almarefh.net\show-content.

55- Miqdad Yaljehin. (1992). (Ethical Education in Islam). Encyclopedia of Islamic Ethics. Dar Alam Al Kotob for Publishing - Riyadh.

56- Wayne Walter Dyer. (D.T). (How to Achieve Your Desires in Special Way), translated by Jarir library.

57- Edwardes, Pawl, ed. (1967). Encyclopcdia of philosophy, New York. Macmilan. comp. vol 3

58- Frankcna. w ,(1963), ethics, Print ice – hall. In . New York.

59- Stock, J. Morality and Purpose. (1969). Routledge and kegan– Paul, London.

60- Could J & Kolb, (1964), dictionary of the social Science, N.Y., Free Press.

Table of content

- Appendixes (National Strategy for Protecting Integrity and Combating Corruption)

Appendixes

Kingdom of Saudi Arabia

Bureau of Experts at the Council of Ministers

National Strategy for Protecting Integrity

and

Combating Corruption

Issued by Council of Ministers resolution

(43) on 01\02\1428 A.H

Saudi Laws Translation

In English

First Edition 1432 A.H

IN THE NAME OF ALLAH, THE MOST GRACIOUS, THE MOST MERCIFUL

No.: (43)

Date: 01\02\1428 AH

The Council of Ministers

After reviewing the conduct of the office of the Council of Ministers' Presidency upon the Royal decree No. (6487\ M B) on 02\09\1427 AH, including a letter from His Highness, the Minister of Interior, with the number 2sh\10889\16 and dated 20\02\1426 AH, attached therewith the report of the Ministerial Committee formed upon the Royal decree No. (5657\B\7) on 09\05\1421 AH, concerning the project of the National Strategy for Protecting Integrity and Combating Corruption.

After the review of the report No. (175) dated 23\02\1424H and organized in the committee of Experts, hearing the Resolution of the Shura Council No. (3\4) on 13\03\1425 AH, reviewing the recommendation No. (733) on 27\11\1427 AH of the Council of Ministers' General Committee,

The Council concluded:

Approving the National Strategy for Protecting Integrity and Combating Corruption in the attached form.

Prime Minister...

<u>**National Strategy for Protecting Integrity and Combating Corruption**</u>

<u>**Introduction:**</u>

Praise be to Allah alone. Peace and blessings of Allah be upon his last Prophet, all of the prophet's folks and companions…

Corruption is considered to be a combined concept with several dimensions whose definitions vary according to the angle you look through.

Every act violating the rules and controls imposed by the system and threatens the public interest by abusing it to earn an individual interest is corrupt according to laws, while in the Islamic Sharia law, corruption is everything against goodness and fair. Allah Almighty said in Quran- Sura "Al-A'raf (56)

{And cause not corruption upon the earth after its reformation} "Allah Also said" **{Indeed, Allah commands you to render trusts to whom they are due and when you judge between people to judge with justice. Excellent is that which Allah instructs you. Indeed, Allah is ever Hearing and Seeing}** (AN-Nisa- 58), Allah Also said **{When he turns his back, His aim everywhere is to spread mischief through the earth and destroy crops and cattle. But Allah loveth not mischief}** AL- Baqarah (205) In Sahih Muslim (Imam Muslim's correct Book of Hadith), The Messenger of Allah- PBUH- said:

"There is none amongst the bondsmen who was entrusted with the affairs of his subjects and he died in such a state that he was dishonest in his dealings with those over whom he ruled that the Paradise is not forbidden for him."

Imam Ahmed said, Thawban said, "The Messenger of Allah- PBUH- cursed the one who offers the bribe, the one who receives it, and the one who arranges it.

The phenomenon of corruption includes several crimes such as:

Bribery, illicit gain, abuse of power, embezzlement, money laundering, accountancy crimes, forgery, forgery of money, commercial fraud, etc.

Countries' experiences, regardless of the level of their economic development or regime, indicate that corruption is not relevant to a certain regime. In fact, it appears when the surround environment help it and will be existed in variable and different forms in all regimes as corruption is considered as an international phenomenon and a factor causes the international community worry.

The phenomenon of corruption is considered as a combined phenomenon where economic, social, cultural and political dimensions merge which is why the corruption has many causes to create it Such as, the incoherence of systems, the requirements of social life and the weakness of observation.

Corruption has several negative effects, the top of which is the negative effect on the development, which makes it misconduct its targets, wastes its resources, misleads it, frustrate its process, weakens the effectiveness and efficiency of systems and creates a state of discontent and anxiety.

Protecting Integrity and Combating Corruption require a comprehensive reformation programs, which have a strong political support and obtain a strategic essence based on diagnosing the problem and their causes, cooperation of the governmental authorities, participation of the community and its organizations, advocating and reinforcing the moral values and principles of the authority and the community and benefiting from the international experiences.

Whereas Protecting Integrity and Combating Corruption in all its forms is one of the settled principles in the Islamic Sharia and international laws, while the Kingdom of Saudi Arabia derives its own laws from the principles and rules of Sharia, which Protecting Integrity and Combating Corruption in all its forms.

Consequently, the Kingdom has persisted in sharing the international community's concerns of Anti-corruption through its persistence on holding conventions, attending conferences and discussions, and reinforcing the international cooperation.

In addition, the Kingdom set this strategy for Protecting Integrity and Combating Corruption as follows:

Firstly: The Methods:

The strategy of Protecting Integrity and Combating Corruption is based on the following points:

1- The religion of Islam– is a method of life - and the mean support that governs this strategy's points, targets, means and mechanisms. Every act that would divert the public or the private function from their legal and regular track, the mean function which they were founded to serve, is considered as an corruption or a crime that demand punishment in this world and in the Hereafter.

2-Protecting Integrity and Combating Corruption is appropriately achieved by reinforcing the cooperation among the relevant authorities in the Kingdom.

3-Corruption frustrates development, progress and investments.

Page **166** of **172**

4- Some forms of corruption are associated with criminal activities, especially the organized crime across the national borders.

5- Forming of new concepts and methods of corruption require a continuous review and evaluation for the policies, plans, systems, procedures and programs for combating that serious disease.

6-Achieving the protection of integrity and combating corruption also requires boosting the cooperation among countries in accordance with the principles of international law, conventions and covenants, which aims to increase trust among countries and creating a better atmosphere of the relationships amongst them.

Secondly: The Targets:

The National Strategy for Protecting Integrity and Combating Corruption aims to achieve the following:

1- Protecting the Integrity and Combating Corruption in all its forms.

2- Fortifying the Saudi Community against corruption through the religious, moral and educational values.

3- Guiding citizens and residents towards having the right behavior and the respecting the religious and formal rules.

4- Providing an appropriate atmosphere for the success of the developmental plans, particularly the economic and the social ones.

5-Participating in the efforts exerted in the reinforcement, development and consolidation of regional, Arabian and international cooperation in the field of Protecting Integrity and Combating Corruption.

6- Achieving social equity among the individuals in society.

Thirdly: The Means:

Diagnosing the problem of corruption in the Kingdom by the following:

A- Organizing a national database for Protecting Integrity and Combating Corruption that contains all the formal and administrative documents as well as monitoring the accurate information, data and statistics on the seriousness, nature, classification, definition, causes, impacts and priorities of the problem and the social, timing and regional range of spread.

B- The relevant governmental authorities providing statistics and periodical reports on the problem of corruption that include the seriousness, causes, types and the suggested solutions to the problem as well as define the drawbacks and difficulties which oppose the application of systems and procedures associated with Protecting Integrity and Combating Corruption.

C- Implementing and supporting the studies and researches associated with Protecting Integrity and Combating Corruption.

D- Providing those willing to studying and researching with the available information and urging the academic authorities and the specialized research centers to accomplish more studies and researches in the same field.

E- Monitoring what is being broadcasted in the Media regarding Protecting Integrity and Combating Corruption.

F- Following up the latest developments in this field on the local and international level.

2-The governmental authorities concerned with Protecting Integrity and Combating Corruption's practicing for their authorities and applying the relevant systems by the following:

A- Providing the regulator, investigative and judicial authorities with the sufficient financial and human resources, experiences, training, technology, Modern scientific methods to enable these authorities to perform their tasks effectively.

B- Studying the systems, organizational structure and procedures of the relevant authorities for Protecting Integrity and Combating Corruption with consider to non- duplicity and conflict of competency among them as well as granting them the appropriate administrative and financial independence.

C- The competent governmental authorities to make a periodical audit of the competent Anti-corruption systems to define the difficulties they would face through the application and study as well as providing suggestions to overcome these difficulties and developing these systems and directing them to the competent authorities for reviewing them and making use of   them   at   similar   circumstances.

D- Developing and reforming the regulatory, administrative and financial systems to insure their clarity, applicability and effectiveness.

E- Reducing, facilitating the procedures, awareness the people with it and as well as locate these procedures in major places so that they won't result in informal exclusions.

F- Officials' control and monitoring to insure the correctness of work procedures and their conformity to the systems.

G- Choosing the administrators in the executive departments relating to the public and treating well the auditors in this executive administration. Asserting heads of departments to facilitate citizens' relevant procedures and monitor the employees so that they won't set obstacles for these procedures.

H- Asserting equity in handling regardless of the social or official position of the person.

I- Working according to the principle of questioning any official, according to the systems, regardless of his\ her position.

J- Reinforcing the efforts of the control authorities which related to Combating corruption.

K- Taking advantage of the modern scientific means and fastest means of communication among the competent governmental authorities.

L- Insuring the clarity of the procedures of the fees, claims, fines and their payment and finding the protective means capable of filling the gaps that would result in the corruption's entrance into them, including the payment through banks according to tried controls.

M- Fast settlement of corruption cases, compensating those whose rights and interests were damaged by corruption after that had been proved by a final judicial judgment of the relevant agency that is published upon an order from the general attorney and approval of the case's judge.

N- Working on the unification of the committees of judicial jurisdiction into one judicial authority and granting it complete independence.

O- Asserting cooperation in the mutual assistance for combating corruption, with no violation of bank secrecy.

3- Verifying the principle of clearness (Integrity) and reinforcing it within the state institutions through the following:

A- Asserting on the state officials that clarity is an effective mean for protection from corruption and that adopting it as a practice and a moral orientation that adds credibility and respect to the governmental work.

B- Facilitating and explaining the administrative procedures and making them available on request as well as not resorting to secrecy except with the information associated with the national sovereignty and security.

C- Setting a system for public money protection.

D- Clarifying the procedures of purchase contracts of the government, public institutions and joint stock companies, and granting the public, the civil institution and the media the right to review and criticize those procedures.

E- Granting the freedom for the circulation of information concerning the issues of corruption amongst people and media.

4- Participation of the civil society organizations in protecting the integrity and combating corruption through the following:

A- The involvement of some members of these organizations in the suggested National Commission for Combating Corruption.

B- Involving these organizations "according to their specialization" in the study of the phenomenon of corruption and displaying their opinions and suggestions to reduce it.

C- Urging the occupational and the academic authorities such as doctors, lawyers, engineers and accountants authorities to display their opinions on the (Control, financial and administrative) systems and to make their suggestions on developing and updating those systems.

D- Urging chamber of commerce and industry to set plans and programs to educate the business men and merchants about the hazards, causes and effects of corruption and displaying their opinions on the financial and commercial systems.

5- Public awareness and reinforcement of moral behavior through the following:

A- Improving the religious influence to urge the integrity and combating corruption through the variable media, Preacher in the mosque, and other educational institutions. Furthermore, arranging a national awareness campaign, which warning the people from the disease of corruption.

B- Emphasizing the role of the family in educating the young generation and its fundamental role in establishing a Muslim society for eliminating the corruption.

C- Urging the educational institutions to add items to the educational curricula and the academic education, and implement educational awareness programs on periodical basis concerning Protecting Integrity and Combating Corruption and Abuse of Confidence.

D- Urging citizens and residents to cooperate with the relevant anti-corruption agencies and report corruption crimes and their perpetrators.

E- Working on setting an educational awareness program in the field of Protecting Integrity and Combating Corruption in both public and private sectors.

6-Improving the domestic, job and living conditions of the citizens through the following:

A- Emphasizing the principle of improving the domestic, job and living conditions of the citizens, particularly lower income citizens, and providing them with the fundamental services.

B- Providing job opportunities in (Both public and private sectors) in accordance with the regular increase of population and graduates, and qualifying them according to the needs of the labor market.

C- Limiting Recruitment of foreign workers.

D- Improving the employers' rates of wages, particularly the minimal wages.

7- Reinforcing the Arabian, regional and international cooperation through the following:

A- When committing to a covenant or a convention, the country's national sovereignty shall be taken into account as well as non-intervention in its own internal affairs.

The Kingdom shall have its own effective role in composing the terms of these covenants and conventions.

Besides taking into account the level of commitment and clarity among the developed and the developing countries, and working on making a good choice in selecting the participants so that they are professionals.

B-The importance of the coordination among the agencies participating in the relevant anti-corruption causes, good preparation and arrangement for these participations and working on setting a projection for the Kingdom with regard to the topics being discussed since the issue of corruption is an international issue that is beyond the borders of any country.

C- Taking advantage of the experiences of the countries as well as the international governmental and non-governmental organizations in the field of Protecting Integrity and Combating Corruption.

D- Following up the latest international developments about corruption and bribery crimes, and the means of detecting and besieging them.

E-Working on achieving more effective cooperation, mutual legal assistance, exchange of information, opinions and experiences in the field of Protecting Integrity and Combating Corruption with the countries of the Cooperation Council for the Arab States of the Gulf as well as the Arab and Islamic friendly states.

F- The Official Translation Department in the Bureau of Experts at the Council of Ministers established under Council of Ministers Resolution No. 134 dated 02\05\1422 AH shall give the priority to the translation of relevant anti-corruption systems applied in the Kingdom into foreign living languages so as to be useful for foreign participations concerning Combating corruption and signify the Kingdom's attitude and efforts towards that cause.

Fourthly: The Mechanisms:

Establishing a National organization for Combating Corruption that takes over the following tasks:

A- Tracking the implementation of the strategy, monitoring its results, evaluating and auditing it, and setting its programs of action and its application's mechanisms.

B- Coordination of the efforts of both the public and the private sectors concerning planning, monitoring and evaluating the anti-corruption systems.

C- Receiving, analyzing and producing analysis Sheet for the periodical reports and statistics of the relevant authorities.

D- Collecting, classifying, assessing, analyzing and exchanging the information, data and statistics with the relevant specialized organizations.

Allah is the arbiter of success,,,